What People Are Saying

"Trusting a recipe often comes down to trusting the source.
The sources for the recipes are impeccable;
in fact, they're some of the best chefs in the nation."
BON APPETIT MAGAZINE

"Should be in the library—and kitchen—of every serious cook."
JIM WOOD—Food & Wine Editor—San Francisco Examiner

"A well-organized and user-friendly tribute to many
of the state's finest restaurant chefs."
SAN FRANCISCO CHRONICLE

"An attractive guide to the best restaurants and inns,
offering recipes from their delectable repertoire of menus."
GAIL RUDDER KENT—Country Inns Magazine

"Outstanding Cookbook"
HERITAGE NEWSPAPERS

"I couldn't decide whether to reach for my telephone and make reservations
or reach for my apron and start cooking."
JAMES MCNAIR—Best-selling cookbook author

"It's an answer to what to eat, where to eat—and how to do it yourself."
THE HERALD

"I dare you to browse through these recipes
without being tempted to rush to the kitchen."
PAT GRIFFITH—Chief, Washington Bureau, Blade Communications, Inc.

Books of the "Secrets" Series

THE GREAT VEGETARIAN COOKBOOK

COOKING SECRETS FOR HEALTHY LIVING

THE GREAT CALIFORNIA COOKBOOK

CALIFORNIA WINE COUNTRY COOKING SECRETS

SAN FRANCISCO'S COOKING SECRETS

MONTEREY'S COOKING SECRETS

PACIFIC NORTHWEST COOKING SECRETS

NEW ENGLAND'S COOKING SECRETS

CAPE COD'S COOKING SECRETS

THE GARDENER'S COOKBOOK

JEWISH COOKING SECRETS

GUIDEBOOK & COOKBOOK

PACIFIC NORTHWEST COOKING SECRETS

Starring the finest restaurants, inns, and wineries of Oregon, Washington and Canada.

Kathleen DeVanna Fish

Library of Congress Cataloging-in-Publication Data

PACIFIC NORTHWEST COOKING SECRETS
The Chefs' Secret Recipes

Fish, Kathleen DeVanna
96-836112
ISBN 1-883214-07-6
$15.95 softcover
Includes indexes
Autobiography page

Cover photograph by Robert N. Fish
Editorial direction by Meredith Phillips, Perseverance Editorial Services
Editorial assistance by Nadine Guarrera
Cover design by Morris Design
Cover styling by Susan Devaty
Illustrations by Krishna Gopa, Graphic Design & Illustration
Type by Electra Typography

Published by Bon Vivant Press
a division of The Millennium Publishing Group
PO Box 1994
Monterey, CA 93942

Printed in the United States of America
by Publishers Press

Contents

The Pacific Northwest

A Brave New World of Food and Wines

The Great Pacific Northwest has become a mecca for lovers of exquisite food and wine. Cultures from all over the world settled in the unique area ranging from the Oregon coast to Washington and into British Columbia. The settlers brought cuisines, methods and tastes from all over the world. They discovered a land rich with seafood, fruits, produce and wild game. And they developed a wine region that is tempting palates all over the world.

Pacific Northwest Cooking Secrets captures the flavors and spirit of the region. It offers you inside information on the best restaurants, inns and wineries—and it reveals the secret recipes of 98 of the region's greatest chefs. You probably will recognize some of the cooking stars. And you will meet a new galaxy of master chefs. None of the chefs paid to be included in this book. They—and their restaurants, inns and wineries—were hand-selected and invited to participate. The requirements: excellence of food, consistency of quality and a flair for beautiful presentation.

The very selective list of restaurants includes some that are elegant, some that are comfortably casual, and some that the locals would prefer to keep secret. The determining factor is fabulous food.

We also include recommendations for unforgettable places to stay. Each inn was chosen because it is so enchanting, so perfect in service and ambience that you will luxuriate in the surroundings. Drawings of each inn by our artist will help you decide where to stay.

The Pacific Northwest offers a rich array of ingredients. The selection of exquisite seafood includes unsurpassed salmon, Dungeness crab, prawns, clams, oysters and mussels. The forest yields exotic mushrooms such as chanterelles and portobellos. Local game includes deer, duck and pheasants. The region abounds in cherries, huckleberries, peaches, grapes, apricots, leeks and potatoes. The possibilities are endless.

You will discover dishes with roots in Native America and the cuisines of France, Mexico, Italy, Scandinavia, China, Japan, Thailand and Vietnam, to name a few. Pacific Northwest chefs can draw from a rich heritage of cooking styles. While the Native Americans often smoked salmon over green alder wood, Swedish cooks prefer to bake their fish. And the Italian chef will often blend salmon with an assortment of local shellfish and vegetables, to create a seafood stew.

We took the chefs' recipes—165 of them—and adapted them for the home cook. Some of the recipes are simple. Some are more complex. We stayed clear of purely trendy food, preferring to stress dishes that we know are wonderful. To make your life easier, we include preparation times and cooking times. And we list the recipes in these handy categories: Breakfast, Appetizers, Soups, Salads and Dressings, Seafood, Poultry, Game, Meats, Main Course, Pasta and Grains, Vegetables and Side Dishes, and Final Temptations.

The 165 kitchen-tested recipes feature such enticing dishes as Baked Strawberry French Toast, Thai Black Rice and Dungeness Crabcakes, Maple and Bourbon Smoked Salmon, Chicken Breasts with Fresh Peaches and Hazelnut Breading, Duck with a Cabernet Cherry Sauce over Angel Hair Pasta, Port Wine Braised Mushrooms, and a Hazelnut Meringue Cake with Chocolate Cinnamon Cream.

Prepare to be tempted.

Chefs' Favorite Recipes

Breakfast and Breads

Appetizers

Soups

Salads and Dressings

Seafood

Poultry

Game

Meat

Main Courses

Pasta & Grains

Vegetables & Side Dishes

Final Temptations

Cooking Stars of the Pacific Northwest

Oregon

Bay House

Greg Meixner

5911 Southwest Highway 101
Lincoln City, Oregon
541-996-3222

Canyon Way Restaurant and Bookstore

Michael Downing

1216 Southwest Canyon Way
Newport, Oregon
541-265-8319

Chateaulin Restaurant and Wine Shoppe

David Taub

50 East Main
Ashland, Oregon
541-482-2264

Chez Jeannette

Andrew Meuller

7150 Old Highway 101
Gleneden Beach, Oregon
503-764-3434

Genoa

Catherine Whims

2832 Southeast Belmont Street
Portland, Oregon
503-238-1464

JARBOE'S IN MANZANITA

KLAUS MONBERG

137 Laneda Avenue
Manzanita, Oregon
503-368-5113

L'AUBERGE

NICOLAS ADAM

2601 Northwest Vaughn Street
Portland, Oregon
503-223-3302

PAZZO RISTORANTE

DAVID MACHADO

627 Southwest Washington
Portland, Oregon
503-228-1212

3 DOORS DOWN

DAVE MARTH

1429 Southeast 37th Avenue
Portland, Oregon
503-236-6886

WILDWOOD RESTAURANT

CORY SCHREIBER

1221 Northwest 21st Avenue
Portland, Oregon
503-248-9663

WASHINGTON

AL BOCCALINO RISTORANTE

DONALD ALCORN AND ANDREW ELARTH

1 Yesler Way
Seattle, Washington
206-622-7688

BAY CAFÉ

ROBERT WOOD

Lopez Town
Lopez Island, Washington
360-468-3700

CHEZ SHEA

PETER MORRISON

94 Pike Street, Suite 34
Seattle, Washington
206-467-9990

FLYING FISH RESTAURANT, BAR AND GRILL

CHRISTINE KEFF

2234 First Avenue
Seattle, Washington
206-728-8595

FULLER'S—SHERATON SEATTLE HOTEL AND TOWERS

MONIQUE ANDRÉE BARBEAU

1400 Sixth Avenue
Seattle, Washington
206-447-5544

Il Bistro

Dino Daquila

93-A Pike Street
Seattle, Washington 98101
206-682-3049

Il Terrazzo Carmine

Carmine Smeraldo

411 First Avenue South
Seattle, Washington
206-467-7797

Le Gourmand

Bruce Naftaly

425 Northwest Mark Street
Seattle, Washington
206-784-3463

Pirosmani

Laura Dewell

2220 Queen Anne Avenue North
Seattle, Washington
206-285-3360

Ponti Seafood Grill

Alvin Binuya

3014 Third North
Seattle, Washington
206-284-3000

RAY'S BOATHOUSE, CAFÉ AND CATERING

CHARLES RAMSEYER

6049 Seaview Avenue Northwest
Seattle, Washington
206-789-3770

ROVER'S

THIERRY RAUTUREAU

2808 East Madison
Seattle, Washington
206-325-7442

TULIO

WALTER PISANO

1100 Fifth Avenue
Seattle, Washington
206-624-5500

UNION BAY CAFÉ

MARK MANLEY

3515 Northeast 45th Street
Seattle, Washington
206-527-8364

BRITISH COLUMBIA

THE ALABASTER RESTAURANT

MARKUS WIELAND

1168 Hamilton Street
Vancouver, British Columbia, Canada
604-687-1758

CAFFE DE MEDICI RESTAURANT

GINO PUNZO

109-1025 Robson Street
Vancouver, British Columbia, Canada
604-669-9322

HERON'S RESTAURANT & LOUNGE

DARYLE RYO NAGATA

900 Canada Place Way
Vancouver, British Columbia, Canada
604-691-1991

LA RÚA RESTAURANTE

TIM MUEHLBAUER

4557 Blackcomb Way
Whistler, British Columbia, Canada
604-932-5011

LE CLUB—THE SUTTON PLACE HOTEL

KAI LERMEN

845 Burrard Street
Vancouver, British Columbia, Canada
604-682-5511

LE CROCODILE

MICHEL JACOB

100-909 Burrard Street
Vancouver, British Columbia, Canada
604-669-4298

Monterey Lounge & Grill—
Pacific Palisades Hotel

Denis Blais

1277 Robson Street
Vancouver, British Columbia, Canada
604-688-0461

Raintree Restaurant at the Landing

Herb Quinn

375 Water Street
Gastown, Vancouver, British Columbia, Canada
604-688-5570

Seasons In the Park Restaurant

Pierre Delâcote

Queen Elizabeth Park Cambie at 33rd
Vancouver, British Columbia, Canada
604-874-8008

Star Anise Restaurant

Julian Bond

1485 West 12th Avenue
Vancouver, British Columbia, Canada
604-737-1485

Tojo's Restaurant

Hidekazu Tojo

202-777 West Broadway
Vancouver, British Columbia, Canada
604-872-8050

Val d'Isère

Roland Pfaff

4433 Sundial Place, Village Center
Whistler, British Columbia, Canada
604-932-4666

Apple Crepes with Cider Sauce

Pacific Northwest Eggs

Baked Strawberry Banana French Toast

Corn Fritters Served with Zesty Salsa

Toasty Homemade Granola

Cappuccino Muffins

Omelet Soufflé à l'Orange

Austrian Pancakes

Chive Popovers

Curry Rice Quiche

Coconut Date Walnut Scones

Spiced Waffles

Apple Crepes with Cider Sauce

Yields: 15 to 18 crepes
Preparation Time:
45 Minutes (note refrigeration time)

1½ cups flour
1½ cup sugar
½ tsp. salt
6 eggs
Grated orange or lemon rind
3 cups milk
10 Granny Smith apples
1 tsp. cinnamon
¼ cup lemon juice
¾ cup melted butter

Cider Sauce
2 cups apple cider
⅓ cup apple vinegar
½ tsp. cinnamon
¼ cup sugar
1 stick butter
Powdered sugar, garnish

In a large mixing bowl combine the flour, ½ cup sugar and salt. Add the eggs, one at a time, beating to produce a perfectly smooth batter. Add the rind and milk, making sure that the batter is without any lumps.

It is important that the batter is prepared at least two hours before using it. The batter may be made the night before, and left in the refrigerator.

Peel, core, and slice the apples. Add the cinnamon, 1 cup sugar and lemon juice. Mix well and let stand overnight, covered with plastic wrap.

Cook the crepes in a very hot pan, lightly brushed with melted butter. The crepes should be thin and golden brown on both sides. Stack them on top of each other, and keep them covered and warm. Makes about 15 to 18 crepes.

In a large pan sauté the apple until soft, but still firm. Set aside.

Cider Sauce

Place the first four ingredients in a saucepan and reduce over medium heat to about ½ cup. Cut the butter into small cubes and slowly add the butter to the sauce, one by one, until the sauce has thickened. Keep warm.

Assemble the crepes on individual plates. Place a heaping Tbsp. of apples in the middle of the crepe, pour 2 to 3 Tbsps. of cider sauce over the apples, fold the crepe in half, sprinkle with some powdered sugar and serve at once.

Gerti and Karl Fuss
The Old Farmhouse
Salt Spring Island, British Columbia

Pacific Northwest Eggs

Serves 6
Preparation Time:
30 Minutes
Pre-heat oven to 350°

- 6 puff pastry shells
- 2 Tbsps. butter
- 1 Tbsp. flour
- ⅔ cup milk
- 1 sprig lemon thyme, chopped
- ¼ cup Parmesan cheese, grated
- Salt and pepper to taste
- 12 whole eggs
- 6 oz. smoked salmon
- 1 small leek or green onion, chopped

Bake the pastry shells according to package directions. Remove tops and inner dough.

To prepare the sauce, melt the butter in a medium-size saucepan and add flour. Add milk gradually, stirring or whisking constantly. Add lemon thyme leaves and parmesan cheese to sauce. Salt and pepper to taste.

Scramble the eggs over medium heat. Remove and spoon scrambled eggs into baked pastry shells, top with Parmesan sauce, smoked salmon and chopped leeks.

COOKING SECRET: Serve this breakfast on a plate with fresh fruit and pansies or other edible flowers from your garden. It makes an elegant meal and an impressive presentation.

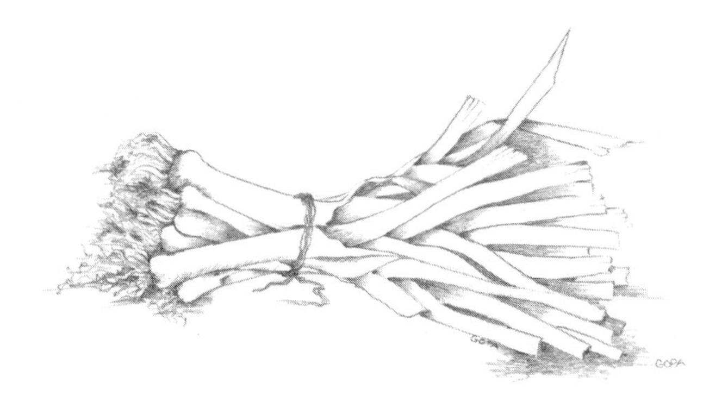

Peggy Kuan
Chanticleer Inn
Ashland, Oregon

Baked Strawberry-Banana French Toast

Serves 4
Preparation Time: 45 Minutes
Pre-heat oven to 400°

- **¾ cup flour**
- **½ cup brown sugar**
- **¼ cup granulated sugar**
- **1 tsp. cinnamon**
- **¾ cup softened butter**
- **¼ cup strawberry preserves**
- **3 large eggs**
- **¾ cup half & half**
- **1 banana**
- **1 tsp. vanilla**
- **⅛ tsp. allspice**
- **½ cup fresh strawberries, sliced**
- **8 slices extra-thick French bread**
- **Strawberries for garnish, optional**
- **Whipped cream for garnish, optional**

To make the streusel topping, place the flour, brown and white sugar, cinnamon and ¼ cup butter in a food processor and process until mixture has crumb texture. Set aside.

To prepare the strawberry butter place the strawberry preserves and ½ cup softened butter in a food processor and process until smooth. Set aside.

To make the French toast mixture, place the eggs, half & half, banana, vanilla, allspice and strawberries in a blender and pulse on medium speed for 3 minutes. Pour the egg mixture into a bowl for dipping. One at a time, completely immerse each piece of bread in the egg mixture, remove, then dip one side of each piece of bread into the streusel. Place slices streusel-side-up close together on a greased baking sheet. Continue with all eight slices. Let stand for at least 20 minutes.

Bake in a 400° oven for 15 to 20 minutes or until golden brown. Spread with strawberry butter immediately after removing from oven. Serve garnished with fanned strawberries and fresh whipped cream.

Kevin Spanier
The Lion and The Rose
Portland, Oregon

Corn Fritters Served with Zesty Salsa

In a large mixing bowl, sift together the cornmeal and flour. Add the beaten eggs, milk, corn, mustard, salt and pepper, red peppers, cheese and basil, stirring until well combined.

Heat a skillet or griddle with a small amount of oil. Spoon the fritter batter to a 3-inch diameter in hot oil and fry until golden brown. The fritters can be fried ahead and kept warm.

Serve with the spoonfuls of the Zesty Salsa recipe that follows. Top with colorful nasturtium flowers.

Zesty Salsa

In a large mixing bowl, combine all ingredients. Allow to stand at least 30 minutes before serving.

Con and Judi Sollid
Beaconsfield Inn
Victoria, British Columbia

Serves 4
Preparation Time:
45 Minutes

- **1 cup cornmeal**
- **1 cup all-purpose flour**
- **4 eggs, beaten**
- **1⅓ cups milk**
- **1¾ cup corn kernels, drained**
- **1 Tbsp. Dijon mustard**
- **Salt and pepper**
- **½ cup roasted red peppers, minced**
- **1 cup grated fontina cheese**
- **2 Tbsps. fresh basil, chopped**
- **Vegetable oil**

Zesty Salsa

- **2 plum tomatoes, seeded and finely diced**
- **½ medium red onion, finely diced**
- **1 Tbsp. fresh cilantro, chopped**
- **2 Tbsps. fresh Italian parsley, chopped**
- **Salt and pepper**
- **¼ cup red or yellow bell pepper, finely diced**
- **Zest and juice of ½ lime or lemon**
- **¼ cup fresh fruit (pineapple, plum, nectarine, mango, papaya, etc.)**
- **Dash of Tabasco**
- **Nasturtium leaves and flowers for garnish, optional**

Toasty Homemade Granola

Yields: 7 to 8 cups
Preparation Time: 45 Minutes
Pre-heat oven to 350°

- **4 cups raw rolled oats**
- **1 cup slivered almonds**
- **½ cup broken pecans**
- **½ cup wheat germ**
- **½ cup sesame seeds**
- **½ cup raw sunflower seeds**
- **⅓ cup shredded coconut**
- **½ cup packed brown sugar**
- **¼ tsp. salt**
- **1 tsp. ground cinnamon**
- **½ tsp. ground nutmeg**
- **1 cup butter, melted**
- **½ cup powdered milk**
- **⅓ cup maple syrup**
- **½ cup golden raisins**
- **½ cup dried currants**
- **1 Tbsp. grated orange peel**

In a hot skillet combine the oats, almonds and pecans and toast on medium-low, stirring constantly for 5 minutes.

Add the wheat germ, sesame seeds, sunflower seeds and coconut and toast for 10 more minutes, stirring constantly. Sprinkle in brown sugar and salt and stir 2 to 5 more minutes.

Add the remaining ingredients and place in a greased baking dish.

Bake in a 350° oven until granola is golden brown and sticks together, about 30 minutes.

Cool, break up and place in airtight container. The granola will store well for up to one month.

Chuck and Laurel Biegert, Jr.
Mt. Ashland Inn
Ashland, Oregon

Cappuccino Muffins

In a large mixing bowl, combine the eggs, oil, buttermilk, coffee and vanilla. Set aside.

Sift all dry ingredients into a separate bowl. Add the chocolate chips.

Add dry mixture to wet and mix quickly. Don't over-mix. Bake 20 to 25 minutes in a 375° oven.

Christopher Brandmeir
Inn at Swifts Bay
Lopez Island, Washington

Yields: 32 muffins
Preparation Time: 45 Minutes
Pre-heat oven to 375°

- 7 eggs
- 1¾ cups oil
- 1 cup buttermilk
- 1 cup strong black espresso (or ¾ cup coffee, ¼ cup coffee flavored syrup)
- 2 tsps. vanilla extract or powder
- ⅔ cup cocoa
- 4 cups white flour
- 1 cup whole wheat flour
- 2 cups brown sugar
- 1½ tsps. baking powder
- 2½ tsps. baking soda
- 2 tsps. salt
- 2 tsps. cinnamon
- ½ tsp. freshly ground nutmeg
- 2 cups chocolate chips

☆

Omelet Soufflé à l'Orange

Serves 4
Preparation Time:
30 Minutes
Pre-heat oven to 400°

- **5 egg yolks**
- **4 Tbsps. sugar**
- **1 Tbsp. Cointreau**
- **1 orange peel, grated**
- **5 egg whites**
- **1 tsp. lemon juice**
- **2 Tbsps. butter**
- **Powdered sugar for garnish**

Beat the egg yolks with 3½ Tbsps. sugar until frothy. Add the Cointreau and the grated peel of an orange.

In a separate bowl, beat the egg whites with the lemon juice until stiff and gently fold into the egg yolk mixture.

Grease an oval oven-proof dish generously with butter and sugar, and pour the egg mixture into the dish. Cut the orange into thin slices and decorate the top of the soufflé with them.

Sprinkle with powdered sugar and bake for 18 minutes in a 400° oven. Serve at once.

Gerti and Karl Fuss
The Old Farmhouse
Salt Spring Island, British Columbia

Austrian Pancakes

In large mixing bowl, stir together the flour and milk. Whisk in ¼ cup of the melted butter with the salt and egg yolks.

In a separate bowl, beat egg whites with the sugar until very stiff. Fold into the batter.

Melt remaining ¼ cup of butter in a 12-inch round cast-iron skillet. Pour the batter into the skillet and sprinkle with raisins.

Bake in a 375° oven for 20 minutes or until puffy and golden. Tear apart with two forks. Let stand for 3 to 4 minutes before dusting with powdered sugar and serving with stewed fruit such as plums, prunes or cherries.

COOKING SECRET: Serve in cast-iron skillets for rustic appeal. Or serve on individual dessert plates with fruit compote on the side at teatime.

Legend has it that Emperor Franz Joseph always tore his pancakes into small bits before eating them, so his chef began serving them that way.

Serves 8
Preparation Time:
30 Minutes
Pre-heat oven to 375°

- **2 cups all-purpose flour**
- **1 cup milk**
- **½ cup unsalted butter, melted**
- **Pinch of salt**
- **4 eggs, separated**
- **¼ cup granulated sugar**
- **½ cup raisins**
- **Powdered sugar, as needed**
- **Stewed plums or other fruit**

Erika and Peter Durlacher
Durlacher Hof
Whistler, British Columbia

☆

Chive Popovers

Yields: 8 to 10
Preparation Time: 45 Minutes
Pre-heat oven to 450°

- **4 eggs**
- **1½ cups milk**
- **1½ cups flour**
- **½ tsp. salt**
- **2 Tbsps. fresh chives, chopped**
- **Corn oil for the popover pans**

Place the eggs and milk in a food processor and blend. While the food processor is running, add the flour, salt and chopped chives.

Place the corn oil in the bottom of a popover pan or muffin tin and put in the preheated oven for 1 to 2 minutes for the oil to heat up.

Fill the tins half-full with the popover batter and return to the oven for 30 minutes or until the popovers are puffed and golden brown.

Serve immediately.

John and Sherita Weisinger
Weisinger's of Ashland Vineyard and Winery
Ashland, Oregon

Curry Rice Quiche

Place the eggs, cottage cheese, sour cream, onion and garlic powder, curry, baking powder and flour in a blender or food processor. Blend or process on medium speed for two minutes.

Pour the mixture into a mixing bowl and stir in the jack cheese and cooked rice.

Spray 10-inch pie pan with a non-stick vegetable spray. Bake in a 375° oven for 35 to 40 minutes.

Kevin Spanier
The Lion and The Rose
Portland, Oregon

Serves 8
Preparation Time:
45 Minutes
Pre-heat oven to 375°

8 large eggs
½ cup cottage cheese
¼ cup sour cream
1 tsp. onion powder
1 tsp. garlic powder
⅛ tsp. curry
1 tsp. baking powder
¼ cup all-purpose flour
2 cups jack cheese, grated
1 cup cooked long grain rice

Coconut Date Walnut Scones

Serves 4
Preparation Time:
45 Minutes
Pre-heat oven to 375°

4½ cups flour
½ cup sugar
3 Tbsps. baking powder
2½ tsps. salt
1 cup coconut
1 cup dates, chopped
1 cup walnuts, chopped
1 stick butter, 4 oz.
3 eggs, beaten
1¼ cup milk

Stir together the flour, sugar, baking powder and salt in a large mixing bowl. Add the coconut, dates, and walnuts. Cut in the butter until the mixture resembles coarse crumbs. Add the beaten eggs and milk; stir until the dough clings together. Knead gently 12 to 15 times on a lightly floured board.

Cut dough into fourths and form a patted-down square from each part, about ½-inch thick. Cut each square diagonally twice to form four triangles. These triangles can be placed on a sheet and frozen until ready to bake. Thaw to room temperature prior to baking.

Place triangles that you wish to bake on ungreased baking sheet. Bake at 375° until golden brown 12 to 15 minutes.

Carol McGough
The James House
Port Townsend, Washington

Spiced Waffles

In a mixing bowl beat the egg whites until they hold stiff but not dry peaks. Set aside.

In a separate large mixing bowl combine the buttermilk with the melted butter. Add the dry ingredients to the buttermilk mixture and blend until just moistened. Fold in beaten egg whites.

Bake in a pre-heated waffle iron according to manufacturer's directions. Serve with warmed honey or maple syrup and butter.

Yields: Four 6-inch waffles
Preparation Time: 30 Minutes

- **3 egg whites**
- **2 cups buttermilk**
- **½ cup (1 stick) melted butter or margarine**

Blend together:

- **½ cup whole wheat flour**
- **½ cup unbleached white flour**
- **¼ cup rolled oats**
- **¼ cup currants**
- **½ tsp. cinnamon**
- **½ tsp. nutmeg**
- **½ tsp. allspice**
- **½ tsp. salt**
- **2 tsp. baking powder**
- **¾ tsp. soda**

Bill and Susan Fletcher
Turtleback Farm Inn
Eastsound, Washington

Chicken Drumsticks with Merlot & Blackberries

Honeyed Teriyaki Chicken Nuggets

Dungeness Crab and Basil Rolls with Spicy Tomato Coulis

Thai Black Rice and Dungeness Crabcakes

Artichoke Crostini

Eggplant Caviar

Salmon Gravlax

Blue Cheese Meatballs

Scallop Mousse with Chardonnay

Mussels with Saffron & Tomato

Oysters in Red Wine

Arabian Shrimp Paté with Cardamom Cornmeal Waffles

Scallops with Sweet Corn and Walla Walla Onion

Scampi Sautéed with Garlic, Roma Tomatoes, Basil and Vermouth

Thai Red Curry Seafood Purses

Chèvre and Sun-Dried Tomato Tart

Tuna Tartare Infused with Sesame Oil

Chicken Drumsticks with Merlot and Blackberries

lace the drumsticks in a buttered baking dish. Pour ¼ cup of wine over the chicken, sprinkle with paprika, thyme, salt and pepper.

Bake in a 375° oven for 15 minutes.

Remove chicken from oven and baste with ¼ cup Merlot. Return the chicken to the oven for an additional 10 minutes.

Combine the brown sugar, blackberry jam, cumin, garlic, olive oil, and vinegar. Cover the drumsticks on all sides with half of the blackberry mixture using a pastry brush. Return to the oven for another 10 minutes.

Spoon remaining blackberry mixture over the drumsticks before serving.

Serves 4
Preparation Time:
45 Minutes
Pre-heat oven to 375°

- **3 to 4 lbs. chicken drumsticks**
- **½ cup Merlot**
- **1 tsp. paprika**
- **1½ tsp. thyme leaves**
- **Salt and pepper to taste**
- **2 Tbsps. brown sugar**
- **½ cup seedless blackberry jam**
- **½ tsp. ground cumin**
- **2 garlic cloves, minced**
- **1 tsp. olive oil**
- **2 Tbsps. white wine vinegar**

John and Louise Rauner
Yakima River Winery
Prosser, Washington

☆

Honeyed Teriyaki Chicken Nuggets

Serves 4
Preparation Time: 30 Minutes

- **½ tsp. salt**
- **⅛ tsp. pepper**
- **½ cup flour**
- **2 lbs. chicken breasts cut into 2-inch chunks**
- **2 eggs, beaten**
- **Oil for frying**
- **⅓ cup soy sauce**
- **⅓ cup honey**
- **1 Tbsp. dry red wine**
- **1 garlic clove**
- **1 tsp. fresh ginger, grated**

Combine the salt, pepper and flour in a medium plastic bag and shake to blend.

Dip the chicken into beaten egg, then drop into the plastic bag and shake well to coat with seasoned flour.

Heat the oil until hot and add the chicken to fill pan. Cook, turning as needed, until chicken is golden brown, about 5 to 8 minutes depending on size of chicken chunks.

While the chicken is cooking, heat the soy, honey, red wine, garlic and ginger in a small saucepan, until the ingredients are warm and blended together.

When the chicken is cooked crisp and golden brown, remove from the skillet and drain on paper towels. Dip in honey mixture to coat well, then put on a boiler pan or a rack set into a baking pan. Bake at 250° for 20 minutes, brushing with glaze after 10 minutes.

This easy recipe for chicken can be served at room temperature as an appetizer or hot for dinner. Experiment with different wines for different foods, don't get stuck in the "white wine with chicken and red wine with red meat" rut.

Pam and Joel Tefft
Tefft Cellars
Outlook, Washington

Dungeness Crab and Basil Rolls with Spicy Tomato Coulis

In a medium-sized saucepan, boil the rice stick noodles in lightly salted water until al dente, 3 to 5 minutes. Rinse with cold water and drain thoroughly.

Transfer to a mixing bowl and add the crab, finely chopped lemon zest, ½ Tbsp. minced garlic, and one bunch of chopped fresh basil. Mix gently and season to taste with salt, pepper, and a squeeze of lemon juice. Place in the refrigerator while making the sauce.

Purée the tomatoes in a blender or food processor with ½ Tbsp. garlic and olive oil. Season to taste with salt and pepper. Add the jalapeños.

Soften the rice paper wrappers in very hot tap water one at a time. Lay a softened wrapper out on a clean towel and place a portion of the crab-noodle filling at the bottom edge of the wrapper. Fold the two sides inward so they slightly overlap. Roll the folded wrapper toward the top to snugly enclose the filling. Place the completed roll on a tray and continue rolling in the same manner until all the filling is used.

Cover the center of each plate with 2 to 3 Tbsps. of the sauce and place 2 to 3 rolls on the sauce. Garnish with fresh basil and sprinkle of lemon zest.

Serve with a chilled Pinot Gris or Gewürztraminer.

COOKING SECRET: The rolls and sauce may be made up a day in advance, tightly wrapped and refrigerated.

Greg Higgins of Higgins Restaurant and Bar
Montinore Vineyards
Portland, Oregon

Serves 6
Preparation Time:
45 Minutes

1 package rice stick noodles
1½ lbs. fresh Dungeness crab meat
Zest and juice of one lemon
1 Tbsp. minced garlic
2 bunches fresh basil
3 tomatoes, peeled and seeded
2 Tbsps. olive oil
1 jalapeño, roasted, peeled, de-seeded, minced
1 package rice paper spring roll wrappers, 10-inch diameter
Lemon zest for garnish
Basil for garnish
Salt and pepper to taste

Thai Black Rice and Dungeness Crab Cakes

Serves 4
Preparation Time:
40 Minutes

- **1 lb. Dungeness crab meat**
- **2 cups cooked Thai black rice, room temperature**
- **1 yellow or red bell pepper, finely minced**
- **1 Tbsp. grated lime zest**
- **¼ cup fresh basil, chopped**
- **3 Tbsps. fresh mint, chopped**
- **1 Tbsp. fish sauce**
- **1 Tbsp. sesame oil**
- **2 eggs, beaten**
- **¼ cup dry coarse bread crumbs**
- **2 Tbsps. vegetable oil for frying**

In a large bowl, combine the crab meat, black rice, bell peppers, lime zest, basil, mint and fish sauce. Set aside.

Stir the sesame oil into the beaten eggs. Add the oil-egg mixture and bread crumbs to the crab meat and gently stir to combine.

Using a tablespoon of the mixture at a time, form into small cakes about 2 inches in diameter.

Heat the vegetable oil in a large nonstick skillet over medium heat. Working in batches, cook the crab cakes until browned and firm, about 2 minutes per side.

COOKING SECRET: Thai black rice is available in Asian markets.

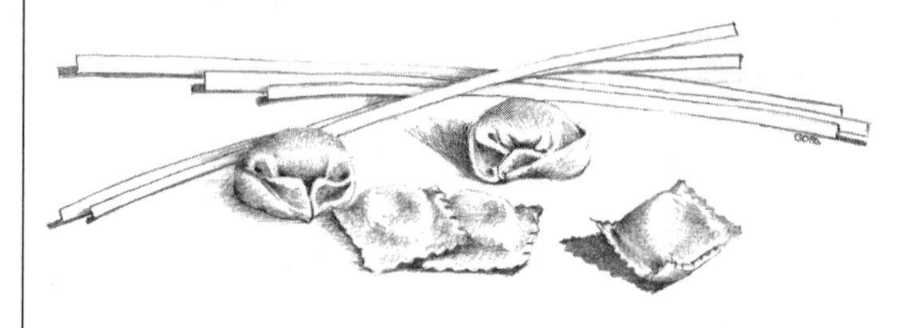

Robert Wood
Bay Café
Lopez Island, Washington

Artichoke Crostini

Serves 8
Preparation Time:
45 Minutes
Pre-heat the oven to 400°

- 2 red bell peppers
- Olive oil
- 4 Tbsps. unsalted butter, room temperature
- 2 Tbsps. fresh flat-leaf parsley, finely chopped
- 2 garlic cloves, crushed through a press
- Salt and freshly ground pepper
- 24 slices of French bread, ¼ inch thick
- 1 lemon, halved
- 4 medium artichokes
- ¼ lb. provolone or mozzarella cheese, thinly sliced or shaved into 24 pieces

Roast the bell peppers directly over a gas flame or under a broiler as close to the heat as possible, turning often until charred all over. Using tongs, transfer the peppers to a paper bag and set aside to steam for 10 minutes. Using a small sharp knife, scrape off the blackened skins and remove the stems, seeds, and ribs. Cut the peppers into 1 by 2 inch strips. Drizzle with olive oil. (The peppers can be prepared to this point up to 2 days ahead, covered with plastic wrap and refrigerated).

In a small bowl, combine the butter, parsley, garlic and a pinch each of salt and pepper. Evenly spread the garlic butter on the bread slices. Arrange the slices on a baking sheet and toast in a 400° oven for 8 to 10 minutes or until golden brown. Do not turn off the oven.

Fill a medium-sized bowl with water. Squeeze the juice from the lemon halves into the bowl. Reserve the lemon. Prepare 1 artichoke at a time. Trim the artichoke by first removing the 5 or 6 layers of tough outer leaves, bending them back at the base so that they snap off. Trim off the stem. Cut off the top half of the artichoke and discard. Trim away all the dark green parts from the base. Pull off the sharp inner leaves and scoop out the hairy choke with a spoon. Rub all the cut surfaces with reserved lemon halves and place the artichoke heart in the lemon water. Repeat with the remaining artichokes. Cut each artichoke heart into slices, about 1 inch thick.

To assemble the crostini, cover each toasted bread slice with 1 artichoke slice and 1 red pepper strip. Cover the red pepper completely with 1 slice of cheese. Place the crostini on a baking sheet and bake on the top shelf of the oven for 5 minutes, or until the cheese starts to bubble. Serve at once.

Dick Erath
Erath Vineyards
Dundee, Oregon

Eggplant Caviar

Serves 4
Preparation Time:
20 Minutes (note marinating time)
Pre-heat oven to 375°

- **2 eggplants**
- **1 Tbsp. garlic, minced**
- **2 Tbsps. capers**
- **¼ cup diced tomatoes**
- **¼ cup roasted red peppers**
- **2 Tbsps. fresh basil, chopped**
- **½ tsp. ground cumin**
- **⅛ tsp. crushed chiles**
- **Kosher salt and black pepper**
- **Bruschetta**

Marinated Roma Tomatoes

- **3 Roma tomatoes**
- **1 Tbsp. balsamic vinegar**
- **2 Tbsps. olive oil**
- **Pinch of ground pepper**

Slice eggplants in half lengthwise and then each half-slice into thirds, lengthwise. Place the eggplant on a sheet pan. Drizzle with olive oil and season with salt and pepper.

Roast in oven at 375° for 10 to 15 minutes or until the flesh becomes dark brown. Let cool, then scrape eggplant flesh from the skin and place in food processor with the remaining ingredients and purée until smooth. Check seasoning.

Serve on bruschetta and top with marinated Roma tomato slices.

Marinated Roma Tomatoes

Slice the tomatoes and place in a small mixing bowl. Add the vinegar, oil and pepper. Toss and let marinate for at least 30 minutes before using.

Greg Meixner
Bay House
Lincoln City, Oregon

Salmon Gravlax

Remove any bones from the salmon. Line a counter surface or pastry board with waxed paper.

Place the salmon on a cutting board. Using a very sharp slicing knife, start at the large end and slice ⅛-inch thick slices toward the tail. Lay all the slices on waxed paper.

Combine the sugar, salt and dill and sprinkle evenly over the salmon slices. Drizzle the cognac over the fish.

Place the salmon on a platter lined with plastic wrap, cover with more plastic wrap, and refrigerate.

Refrigerate for 2 to 3 days to cure the salmon while retaining its fresh flavors and firmness. Cure it for 4 to 6 days if you prefer a more cured, less firm version.

Serve with thinly sliced English cucumber and fresh dill garish. We suggest serving this with Cooper Mountain Vineyards Pinot Gris.

Jack Duey
Cooper Mountain Vineyards
Beaverton, Oregon

Serves 8
Preparation Time:
10 Minutes (note refrigeration time)

3 lbs. salmon filet, with the skin on
1 Tbsp. sugar
1¾ Tbsps. sea salt
1 Tbsp. dill weed, dried
4 Tbsps. cognac
1 English cucumber, sliced thin
Dill weed sprigs, garnish

Blue Cheese Meatballs

Yield: 75 bite-size meatballs
Preparation Time: 30 Minutes
Pre-heat oven to 350°

- **1 lb. lean ground beef**
- **6 oz. blue cheese, crumbled**
- **1 tsp. salt, optional**
- **1 small clove garlic, minced**
- **½ cup bread crumbs**
- **¼ tsp. oregano**
- **¼ tsp. rosemary**
- **2 Tbsps. parsley, chopped**
- **¾ cup Yakima River Pinot Gris**
- **¼ cup oil**

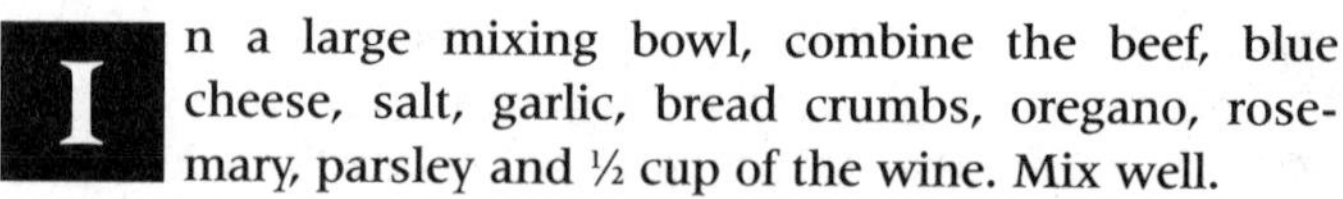

In a large mixing bowl, combine the beef, blue cheese, salt, garlic, bread crumbs, oregano, rosemary, parsley and ½ cup of the wine. Mix well.

Shape mixture into small, bite-size balls (about 1 tsp. each).

Brown the meatballs well on all sides in oil over medium heat. Remove from heat and drain meatballs on paper towels. Refrigerate until ready to use.

Prior to serving, place the meatballs in a shallow casserole or chafing dish. Add the remaining ¼ cup wine and bake in a 350° oven for 15 minutes or until heated through.

These meatballs can be made larger and served as a main dish with spaghetti.

John and Louise Rauner
Yakima River Winery
Prosser, Washington

Scallop Mousse with Chardonnay

Dissolve the gelatin in the clam juice. Set aside

Place the scallops into a food processor and gradually add the clam juice. Add the salt, pepper, Worcestershire sauce, dill, cayenne and paprika and pureé the mixture.

Transfer the scallop mixture into a stainless steel bowl. Add the mayonnaise and Chardonnay. Mix well with a large spoon. When mixture has partially congealed, fold in the whipped cream. Pour into a mold and chill to set.

Serve mousse with crackers and/or baguette slices.

Jack Duey
Cooper Mountain Vineyards
Beaverton, Oregon

Serves 8
Preparation Time:
25 Minutes (note refrigeration time)

- **1½ Tbsps. gelatin powder, unflavored**
- **½ cup clam juice**
- **1 lb. scallops, cooked**
- **1 tsp. sea salt**
- **⅛ tsp. white pepper**
- **1 dash Worcestershire sauce**
- **1 Tbsp. dill**
- **⅛ tsp. cayenne**
- **⅛ tsp. paprika**
- **½ cup mayonnaise**
- **¼ cup Chardonnay**
- **½ cup heavy whipping cream, whipped**

☆

Mussels with Saffron and Tomato

Serves 4
Preparation Time:
30 Minutes

1 pinch saffron
½ cup white wine vinegar
½ cup extra-virgin olive oil
1 cup vegetable oil
Salt and pepper to taste
4 lbs. mussels
½ cup sun-dried tomatoes, cut in thin slices
2 shallots, cut in thin slices
1 Tbsp. garlic, finely minced
Juice of 1 lemon
½ cup Italian parsley, chopped
Sourdough bread, sliced and toasted, rubbed with garlic

In a saucepan over low heat, combine the saffron threads with the vinegar until well blended. Allow to cool. Whisk in the oils and season to taste with salt and pepper. Set aside.

Place the mussels in a heavy-gauge pot or pan large enough so the mussels just cover the bottom. Add the saffron vinaigrette, tomatoes, shallots and garlic. Cover the pot with a tightly fitting lid and place on high heat. As mussels open, remove them so they don't overcook.

When the mussels are open, taste the vinaigrette/broth. Add the lemon juice as desired. Add the parsley leaves and pour hot broth over the mussels.

Serve immediately with sourdough bread.

Cory Schreiber
Wildwood Restaurant
Portland, Oregon

Oysters in Red Wine

Heat 1 Tbsp. oil in a saucepan over medium heat. Add the shallots and garlic and cook until translucent, about 4 minutes. Sprinkle in the sugar and cook, stirring constantly, until the shallots and garlic are golden brown, about 3 minutes. Pour in the wine and season the sauce with half the rosemary, fennel seed and thyme. Cook the sauce until only 1 Tbsp. of liquid remains.

While the sauce is cooking, mix the remaining rosemary, fennel seeds and thyme in a small bowl with the bread crumbs, scallions and a generous grinding of black pepper. Set aside.

Drain the oysters, reserving the liquid. Pour the oyster liquid into the sauce, stirring well to dissolve any caramelized juices on the sides of the pan. Continue cooking the sauce until only ½ cup remains.

Combine the sauce with the oysters and spoon the mixture into an oiled gratin dish. Sprinkle the bread crumb topping over the dish and drizzle the remaining Tbsp. of oil over it.

Bake until top is lightly browned and the oysters are cooked, about 10 minutes. Serve immeadiately.

Tom and Wendy Kreutner
Autumn Wind Vineyard
Newberg, Oregon

Serves 4
Preparation Time:
30 Minutes
Pre-heat oven to 450°

- **2 Tbsps. virgin olive oil**
- **½ cup shallots, finely chopped**
- **4 cloves garlic, finely chopped**
- **1 tsp. sugar**
- **1 cup red wine**
- **1 tsp. fresh rosemary, crushed, or ¼ tsp. dried**
- **½ tsp. fennel seeds, crushed**
- **1½ tsps. fresh thyme, or ½ tsp. dried**
- **½ cup bread crumbs**
- **3 scallions, trimmed and finely chopped**
- **Freshly ground black pepper**
- **1 pt. shucked oysters, with their liquid**

Arabian Shrimp Pâté with Cardamom Cornmeal Waffle

Serves 6
Preparation Time:
20 Minutes (note refrigeration time)

1 lb. fresh shrimp, peeled and deveined
3 Tbsps. butter
Juice of 2 lemons
½ cup fresh bread crumbs
¼ cup Kalamata olives, pitted
½ cup toasted pine nuts
2 Tbsps. fresh parsley, chopped
2 Tbsps. capers, drained
2 cloves fresh garlic, chopped
½ tsp. ground ginger
½ tsp. ground turmeric
½ tsp. ground cumin
1 tsp. ground pasilla chili powder
Salt to taste

In a medium frying pan, fry the shrimp in 1 Tbsp. of butter until just cooked. Add the lemon juice to the hot shrimp and stir.

Transfer the shrimp and remaining ingredients to the bowl of a food processor fitted with the chopping blade. Process the mixture by pulsing until completely smooth.

Transfer the mixture to a lightly oiled one-quart pâté tureen. Chill for two hours before serving.

To serve, run a knife around the edge of the tureen and invert onto a serving platter. Offer the waffles separately.

COOKING SECRET: This simple to prepare pâté is an excellent appetizer and delightful when paired with lightly steamed carrots dressed with melted butter, brown sugar, ginger and cinnamon. Add a bowl of Kalamata olives, sliced cucumbers and the cardamom cornmeal waffles, and you have a nice light meal or after-theater snack.

Robert Wood
Bay Café
Lopez Island, Washington

☆

Cardamom Cornmeal Waffles

In a large mixing bowl, combine the flour, cornmeal, cardamom, baking powder and sugar. Set aside.

In a separate bowl, mix together the quinoa, chives, buttermilk, corn oil and eggs.

Add the wet ingredients to the dry ingredients and mix well to combine.

Pre-heat the oven to 200° and turn on the waffle iron. Spray the waffle iron surfaces with vegetable spray or brush lightly with vegetable oil.

Cook the waffles until lightly browned in the waffle iron. Cut the waffles into wedges and transfer to a sheet pan. Place the cooked waffles in the oven and bake at very low heat for 20 to 30 minutes or until crisp.

COOKING SECRET: These waffles can be made several days in advance if stored in an airtight container. If the waffles seem limp, crisp in the oven for a few minutes at 250°.

Robert Wood
Bay Café
Lopez Island, Washington

Yield: 6 waffles, 24 wedges
Preparation Time:
35 Minutes
Pre-heat oven to 200°

1½ cups flour
½ cup yellow cornmeal, finely ground
2 tsps. ground cardamom
1 tsp. baking powder
1 tsp. sugar
½ cup quinoa, cooked, drained
½ cup fresh chives, finely chopped
¼ cup buttermilk
2 Tbsps. corn oil
6 eggs

Scallops with Sweet Corn and Walla Walla Onions

Serves 4
Preparation Time:
25 Minutes

- **2 Tbsps. olive oil**
- **4 Tbs. pancetta, diced**
- **½ cup onion, diced, (preferably Walla Walla onions)**
- **1 tsp. fresh thyme, chopped**
- **1 lb. large sea scallops (about 16 scallops)**
- **½ cup fresh yellow corn, cut from the cob**
- **2 tsps. garlic, freshly minced**
- **1 cup cherry tomatoes (red or yellow), sliced in half**
- **1 cup white wine**
- **4 Tbsps. butter**
- **Freshly ground pepper to taste**
- **Thyme leaves, garnish**
- **Lemon slices, garnish**

Heat the olive oil in a sauté pan. Add the pancetta, onions and thyme. Cook on high, stirring frequently, until brown. Reduce the heat and add the scallops, corn and garlic. Cook until the scallops are opaque, 3 to 4 minutes, being careful not to brown garlic. Do not overcook the scallops.

Remove the scallops from the pan to warm plates. Set aside.

Add the cherry tomatoes to the sauté pan, and add the white wine to deglaze pan juices. Whisk in butter and spoon over scallops.

Top with freshly ground black pepper. Garnish with fresh thyme leaves and thinly sliced lemon.

David Marth
3 Doors Down
Portland, Oregon

☆

Scampi Sautéed with Garlic, Roma Tomatoes, Basil and Vermouth

Serves 4
Preparation Time:
30 Minutes

- **2 Tbsps. olive oil**
- **28 prawns, peeled and deveined**
- **1 Tbsp. garlic, finely chopped**
- **2 Roma tomatoes, sliced into rounds**
- **Salt to taste**
- **2 Tbsps. fresh lemon juice**
- **4 oz. dry vermouth**
- **2 Tbsps. butter, soft**
- **2 tsps. fresh oregano, chopped**
- **½ cup loosely packed fresh basil leaves, julienne**
- **Lemon wedges and fresh ground black pepper for garnish**

Heat a large sauté pan on medium-high heat. Add the olive oil. When hot, add the prawns. Cook the prawns on one side.

Add the garlic, tomato slices and salt. When garlic is pale golden, turn the prawns and add the lemon juice and vermouth.

When prawns are cooked and liquid is reduced by half, turn off the heat and finish the sauce by stirring in the butter and fresh herbs.

To serve, divide the prawns on four warmed plates and top each with sauce and tomatoes.

Tom Martino
Il Bistro
Seattle, Washington

Thai Red Curry Seafood Purses

Serves 4
Preparation Time:
45 Minutes

- **4 oz. jumbo prawns, shelled, deveined and coarsely chopped**
- **4 oz. Dungeness crab, chopped**
- **4 oz. sea scallops, coarsely chopped**
- **2 stalks lemongrass, white part only, very finely chopped**
- **1 shallot, finely chopped**
- **2 Tbsps. Thai red curry paste**
- **1 lime, zest and juice**
- **8 egg roll wrappers**
- **8 green onion leaves, green part only, lightly steamed, for icing purses**
- **12 oz. Thai sweet chili sauce**

Combine the first 5 ingredients in a mixing bowl.

In a separate small bowl mix together the red curry paste with the lime juice and zest, then combine this well with the seafood mixture.

Place the egg roll wrappers on a flat surface and fill each wrapper with equal amounts of the mixture. Bring the corners together and form "purses," icing each with a green onion leaf.

Fill a large pot with ¾-inch water, and place a steamer rack inside, bringing the water to a boil. Place purses on the rack, cover, and steam for 10 minutes.

To serve, portion the sweet chili sauce on individual plates and top with two purses.

COOKING SECRET: Thai red curry paste is available in some markets, or all Asian markets. We recommend Taste of Thai brand paste.

Michael Downing
Canyon Way Restaurant
Newport, Oregon

Chèvre and Sun-Dried Tomato Tart

Lightly oil a 7×11″ or 9″ square baking pan with 1 tsp. olive oil. Set aside.

In a mixing bowl combine 2 Tbsps. olive oil with 1 egg and buttermilk. Gently work in the cornmeal, flour, sugar, salt, baking powder, garlic and sun-dried tomatoes with a fork. Do not over-beat.

Pour the crust batter into the baking pan and bake at 375° for 8 to 10 minutes. Remove from oven. Set aside.

Prepare the filling by combining the cream cheese, chèvre and 1 egg in a mixing bowl until well blended.

Spread evenly on baked crust and garnish with the zucchini, Parmesan cheese and herbs. Return to the oven for an additional 10 minutes of baking time.

Serve the tart warm or chilled.

Kay Simon
Chinook Wines
Prosser, Washington

Serves 6
Preparation Time:
45 Minutes
Pre-heat oven to 375°

- **2 Tbsps. + 1 tsp. olive oil**
- **2 eggs**
- **½ cup buttermilk**
- **⅔ cup yellow cornmeal**
- **⅓ cup flour**
- **1 Tbsp. sugar**
- **¼ tsp. salt**
- **¼ tsp. baking powder**
- **1 clove garlic, minced**
- **5 sun-dried tomatoes, drained of oil, diced**
- **2 oz. nonfat cream cheese**
- **4 oz. chèvre (goat's milk cheese)**
- **2 baby zucchini, thinly sliced**
- **1 Tbs. freshly grated Parmesan cheese**
- **2 tsps. finely chopped herbs such as basil or thyme**

Tuna Tartare Infused with Sesame Oil and Mirin on Shiitake and Chickpea Salad

Serves 6
Preparation Time:
25 Minutes (note refrigeration time)

1 lb. fresh ahi or yellowfin tuna, finely diced
Juice of 1 lemon
1½ tsps. olive oil
1 scallion, finely sliced
2 tsps. Ginger, finely grated
Pinch of salt and pepper
2 oz. dark soy sauce
3 oz. mirin or rice wine
¼ cup sesame oil
2 Tbsps. sesame seeds
1 cup chickpeas
8 shiitake mushrooms, sliced and sautéed in olive oil
Cilantro, garnish

In a large mixing bowl combine the tuna with the lemon juice, olive oil, scallions, 1 tsp. ginger, salt and pepper. Shape into twelve 1-ounce patties. Refrigerate.

Prepare the sesame vinaigrette by combining the soy sauce, the remaining ginger, mirin or rice wine, sesame oil and sesame seeds in a mixing bowl. Marinate the chickpeas and shiitake mushrooms with a portion of the vinaigrette.

Serve the tuna tartare with the marinated peas and shiitake mixture. Finish with a fresh cilantro leaf. Drizzle the sesame vinaigrette on the salad and plate.

Louis Gervais
Le Club—Sutton Place Hotel
Vancouver, British Columbia

☆

Soups

Asparagus Soup

Serves 4
Preparation Time:
30 Minutes

- **¼ lb. Jerusalem artichokes, washed, cut into small pieces**
- **2 cups chicken stock**
- **1 lb. asparagus, stems removed**
- **¼ cup crème fraîche**
- **Salt and freshly ground white pepper**

Simmer the artichokes in chicken stock until soft, about 15 minutes.

Add the asparagus spears. Simmer until soft, do not overcook.

Purée the soup in a blender or food processor and return to the pot.

Add the crème fraîche. Add more stock or cream to thin soup if desired.

Season to taste with salt and pepper.

Bruce Naftaly
Le Gourmand
Seattle, Washington

Cantaloupe Soup

Purée the cantaloupe chunks in a food processor with small amount of the wine as needed to blend.

Add the honey and pulse untill blended.

Chill in the refigerator for several hours or overnight.

To serve, pour the soup in bowls and float a mint leaf on each serving.

Marilyn Webb
Bethel Heights Vineyard
Salem, Oregon

Serves 4
Preparation Time:
15 Minutes (note refrigeration time)

- **1 ripe cantaloupe, peeled, seeded, cut into chunks**
- **½ cup Bethel Heights Gewürztraminer**
- **2 Tbsps. honey, or to taste**
- **Mint leaves, garnish**

Northwest Crab or Clam Chowder

Serves 6
Preparation Time:
30 Minutes

4 slices bacon, diced
2 Tbsps. flour
3 cups milk
1 cup potatoes, diced
2 Tbsps. onion, chopped
1 clove garlic, minced
1 cup tomato sauce
¼ tsp. basil
¼ tsp. cumin
¼ tsp. marjoram
¼ tsp. cayenne pepper
2 cups flaked crab meat or minced clams
⅓ cup white wine
Salt and pepper to taste

In a large saucepan or soup pot, sauté the diced bacon. Reserve the bacon pieces for garnish. Pour off all but 1½ Tbsps. bacon drippings.

Sprinkle flour over the bacon drippings in the pan. Cook, stirring, for 3 minutes. Add milk, a little at a time, stirring constantly. Cook until smooth and slightly thickened. Add the diced potatoes and onions, garlic, tomato sauce, basil, cumin, marjoram and cayenne pepper. Cover and simmer 10 minutes.

Add the crab meat or clams, white wine, salt and pepper.

Garnish with bacon pieces, chives or parsley.

COOKING SECRET: Serve this hearty soup with fresh sourdough bread and butter.

Irene and Mark McKinley
Orcas Wine Company
Eastsound, Washington

Cioppino

eat the olive oil in a large soup pot over medium heat. Add the garlic, onions, and zucchini and sauté for 5 to 7 minutes, or until the vegetables are soft.

Stir in the tomatoes, Chardonnay and ¼ cup parsley. Cover and cook on medium heat for 5 minutes.

Add the fish, mussels, and scallops, stirring gently. Cover and cook for another 5 minutes.

Serve soup warm, topped with parsley.

Serves 4
Preparation Time:
30 Minutes

- **2 Tbsps. extra-virgin olive oil**
- **3 cloves of garlic, minced**
- **1 large onion, grated**
- **1 large zucchini, grated**
- **3 large red tomatoes, sliced into thin wedges**
- **½ cup Chardonnay**
- **¼ cup + 2 Tbsp. (for garnish) fresh parsley, chopped**
- **1 lb. firm white fish, cut crosswise in strips 1 inch wide**
- **24 small mussels**
- **1 lb. bay scallops**
- **Salt and pepper to taste**

Doug and Jo Ann Fries
Duck Pond Cellars
Dundee, Oregon

Seafood Cioppino

Serves 4
Preparation Time:
30 Minutes

- **¼ cup fennel, chopped**
- **1 leek, chopped**
- **½ onion, chopped**
- **2 tomatoes, chopped**
- **2 Tbsps. virgin olive oil**
- **Salt and pepper to taste**
- **1 tsp. garlic**
- **Pinch of chili flakes**
- **1 tsp. basil, chopped**
- **1 cup white wine**
- **2 cups fish stock**
- **8 clams**
- **8 mussels**
- **1 cup tomato juice**
- **1 lb. assorted firm fish (salmon, monkfish, roughy, etc.)**
- **1 lobster, cut into quarters**
- **4 prawns**
- **¼ lb. scallops**

In a large stock pot, sauté the fennel, leeks, onions and tomatoes in olive oil. Season with salt and pepper.

Add the garlic, chili, basil and white wine and fish stock.

Bring the soup to a boil and add the clams, mussels and tomato juice, cooking for 1 minute.

Reduce the heat and add the firm fish until the fish is almost cooked. Finally add lobster, prawns and scallops. Reduce soup to a simmer and serve when seafood is cooked through.

Irene Laronde
Wedgewood Hotel
Vancouver, British Columbia

☆

Roasted Garlic and Spring Onion Soup

In a large pot, sweat the onions, leeks and celery in the butter. Add the flour to make a roux.

Slowly add the hot chicken stock mixing thoroughly to prevent lumps. Bring to a boil and let the soup simmer, adding the bay leaves and thyme, for one hour.

Add the cream and roasted garlic, bring to a boil and let simmer for 15 minutes. Take off heat, purée all ingredients together and pass through a sieve. Season with salt and pepper to taste.

Mario Enero
La Rúa Restaurante
Whistler, British Columbia

Serves 10
Preparation Time:
1½ Hours

- **1½ whole onions, cut roughly**
- **1 whole leek, cut roughly**
- **¼ head celery, cut roughly**
- **1 cup butter**
- **¾ cup all-purpose flour**
- **6½ qts. chicken stock, heated**
- **1¼ whole bay leaf**
- **⅛ bunch thyme**
- **2 cups cream**
- **2½ lbs. garlic, roasted whole**
- **Salt and pepper to taste**

Gazpacho

Serves 4
Preparation Time:
30 Minutes

3 large tomatoes, peeled, seeded and chopped
1 28 oz. can pear tomatoes (juice and all)
1 rib celery
1 medium carrot
½ red bell pepper
2 green onions
1 cucumber, peeled and seeded
2 Tbsps. fresh basil leaves, chopped
Juice of 2 medium lemons
1 tsp. Chinese chili-garlic sauce
1 to 2 dashes Worcestershire
Salt and pepper to taste
Sour cream, garnish, optional
Cilantro sprigs, garnish, optional
Shrimps, garnish, optional

In blender or food processor, pulse the tomatoes, celery, carrot, bell pepper, onions, cucumber and basil leaves in small batches until just evenly minced, not too fine. If necessary, adjust the consistency with tomato juice to your liking.

Add the lemon juice, chili-garlic sauce, Worcestershire, salt and pepper.

Top with a dollop of sour cream, chopped fresh cilantro, and bay shrimp if desired.

Alvin Binuya
Ponti Seafood Grill
Seattle, Washington

Lentil Soup

Brown the bacon in soup pot. Add the onions, carrots, celery, leeks and garlic. Cook until the onion is transparent.

Add the lentils, parsley, chicken stock, herbs and spices.

Bring the soup to a boil. Reduce the heat and simmer until the lentils are tender, about 1 hour.

Serve soup hot with freshly grated Parmesan cheese.

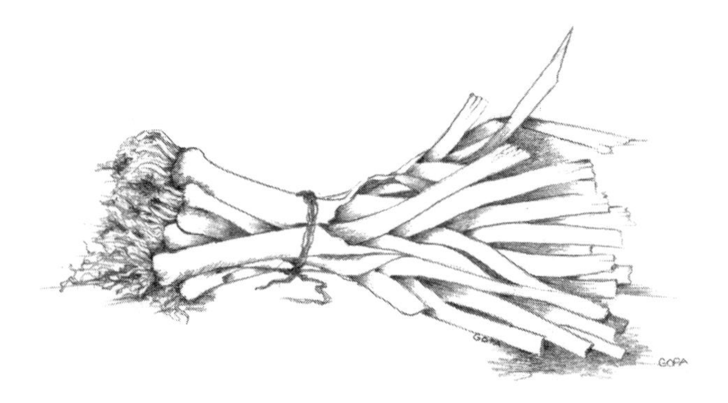

Jerry and Linda Evans
Jacksonville Inn Dinner House
Jacksonville, Oregon

Serves 6
Preparation Time:
1½ Hours

- **¼ lb. bacon, finely diced**
- **1 onion, finely diced**
- **2 carrots, finely diced**
- **2 celery stalks, finely diced**
- **½ leek, finely diced**
- **1 clove garlic, minced**
- **1 cup lentils**
- **¼ cup parsley, chopped**
- **10 cups chicken stock**
- **1 tsp. thyme, ground**
- **1 Tbsp. basil, whole**
- **½ tsp. pepper**
- **1 tsp. salt**
- **Parmesan cheese**

☆

Strawberry Soup with Red Wine

Serves 4
Preparation Time:
30 Minutes

- **1 cup heavy cream**
- **½ vanilla bean**
- **2 egg yolks**
- **¼ cup sugar**
- **3 cups red wine (Pinot Noir is preferable)**
- **2 bay leaves**
- **1 sprig thyme**
- **4 black peppercorns**
- **1 stick cinnamon**
- **4 cloves**
- **½ orange, juice and skin only**
- **½ lemon, juice and skin only**
- **½ Tbsp. ginger, grated**
- **½ cup sugar**
- **2 pts. strawberries, diced (overripe is preferable)**

To prepare the English cream, bring the cream and vanilla bean to a boil in a medium-sized pot over low heat.

In a mixing bowl, beat together the egg yolks and sugar thoroughly and slowly, then add the egg mixture to the boiling cream while whisking. Cook over a low flame until the consistency reaches a light thickness. Cool off quickly.

Place the remaining ingredients, except the strawberries, in a stock pot and bring to a boil. Remove from the flame, cover and let steep for about 10 minutes.

Strain through a fine mesh strainer and reduce the soup to one-third. Cool and mix with the English cream.

Serve soup cold, garnished with the strawberries.

Thierry Rautureau
Rover's
Seattle, Washington

Washington Apple Salad

Asparagus Salad with White Truffle Oil

Beet Salad

Broccoli Salad

Cold Crab Salad with Aioli

Gorgonzola and Pear Salad

Maine Lobster Salad with Citrus and Tomato

Radicchio and Pancetta

Wilted Spinach Salad with Smoked Duck and Bacon

☆

Washington Apple Salad

Serves: 6
Preparation Time:
45 minutes (note marinating time)

- **1 cup dehydrated Washington bing cherries**
- **1 cup semi-sweet white wine**
- **3 medium-size Washington Red Delicious apples**
- **2 medium-size Washington Criterion apples**
- **2 medium-size stalks celery, sliced**
- **1 cup walnuts, chopped**
- **8 oz. Neufchâtel cheese**
- **½ cup half and half**
- **¼ cup granulated sugar**
- **1 Tbps. lemon juice**
- **1 tsp. nutmeg**

Place the cherries in a bowl and cover with wine. Allow to soak at least 30 minutes.

Wash, core and chop apples; do not remove the peel. Combine the apples and celery in large bowl.

Drain cherries and add to apple mixture. Add the walnuts.

In a separate bowl, using a hand mixer, beat the cheese until softened. Add half and half a little at a time until mixture is smooth and of a pouring consistency. Blend in the sugar, lemon juice and nutmeg.

Pour the dressing over the salad and toss to mix. Refrigerate until it is served.

Patty Wolk
Badger Mountain Winery
Kennewick, Washington

Asparagus Salad with White Truffle Oil

Blanch the asparagus in boiling, salted water for 1 minute. Remove and cool under cold running water. Divide asparagus among six plates in a "haystack" style.

Place the tomatoes at the four "corners" of the plate alternating colors, two per plate. Sprinkle corn evenly over the asparagus.

Place the white truffles in a food processor or blender. With the motor running, slowly add the olive oil in a steady stream.

Drizzle dressing liberally over each plate and serve immediately.

COOKING SECRET: The real secret to this dish working so well is the freshness of the ingredients and the pure flavors they give. In early spring we have the actual growers and gatherers come to us with these products. With as little fuss as possible, each item bursts with its own unique flavor and the colors literally jump out at you.

Scot Whigam
RiverPlace Hotel
Portland, Oregon

Serves 6
Preparation Time:
20 Minutes

- **2 lbs. fresh asparagus, trimmed to about 6 inches**
- **12 red and yellow pear tomatoes**
- **1 ear sweet white corn, shucked and cut off the cob**
- **2 fresh white truffles, cleaned**
- **1 cup olive oil**

Beet Salad

Serves 4
Preparation Time:
45 Minutes

- **½ cup raspberry vinegar**
- **1 Tbps. grated orange zest**
- **1 tsp. salt**
- **½ tsp. freshly ground black pepper**
- **1 cup safflower oil**
- **2 bunches fresh beets, steamed until tender**
- **¼ lb. baby lettuce**
- **Blue cheese, garnish**
- **Hazelnuts, toasted, chopped, as garnish**

Whisk together the vinegar, orange zest, salt, pepper, and oil in a mixing bowl. Set the dressing aside.

Peel and julienne the cooked beets. Toss with about ¾ of the dressing.

Arrange lettuce leaves on chilled salad plates and place beet slices over the lettuce. Sprinkle salads with crumbled blue cheese and hazelnuts. Serve remaining dressing separately.

Julie Keppeler
Heron Haus
Portland, Oregon

☆

Broccoli Salad

Serves 10
Preparation Time:
15 Minutes

- **3 broccoli heads, bite sized pieces**
- **½ cup raisins**
- **½ cup red onion, very thinly sliced**
- **½ cup sunflower seeds, optional**
- **1 cup mayonnaise**
- **2 Tbsps. vinegar**
- **2 Tbsps. sugar**
- **4 strips bacon, diced, fried crisp**

In a serving bowl, combine the broccoli, raisins, red onion and sunflower seeds. Set aside.

In a mixing bowl blend the mayonnaise, vinegar and sugar to form dressing and add to the salad.

Just before serving, garnish with the bacon pieces.

Izzy and Nancy Oren
Ponderosa Cattle Company Guest Ranch
Bend, Oregon

Cold Crab Salad with Aioli

Serves 4
Preparation Time:
15 Minutes

- **2 egg yolks**
- **2 garlic cloves, finely chopped**
- **½ Tbsp. Dijon mustard**
- **½ Tbsp. horseradish**
- **6 Tbsps. extra-virgin olive oil**
- **1 tsp. white wine vinegar, optional**
- **2 cups Dungeness crab meat**
- **1 Tbsp. chives, thinly sliced**
- **1 red bell pepper, diced small**
- **1 yellow bell pepper, diced small**
- **½ lb. snow peas, blanched, thinly sliced**
- **2 Tbsps. shallots, chopped**

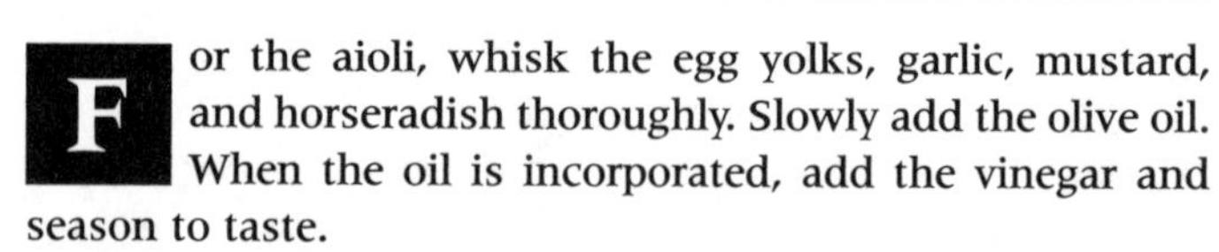

For the aioli, whisk the egg yolks, garlic, mustard, and horseradish thoroughly. Slowly add the olive oil. When the oil is incorporated, add the vinegar and season to taste.

In a salad bowl, mix the crab meat, garnish (red and yellow bell peppers, chives, snow peas, and shallots), and aioli. Season to taste and serve cold.

Thierry Rautureau
Rover's
Seattle, Washington

Gorgonzola and Pear Salad

Place chopped pear in a blender, add the wine and blend thoroughly. Add the oil, 1 tablespoon at a time, until the purée feels "silky" in the mouth. Too much oil affects the taste; use as little as possible. Set aside.

Mix the baby greens, pepper, onion, and the 1 sliced pear in the salad bowl. Dress the salad with the pear purée and toss so that it is just well-coated. Crumble the Gorgonzola over the salad, sprinkle in the nuts and toss again.

COOKING SECRET: The riper the pears, the more flavorful the salad.

Serves 6
Preparation Time:
25 Minutes

- **2 large ripe Bartlett pears (one peeled, one cored)**
- **¼ cup Late Harvest Riesling wine**
- **2 to 3 Tbsps. vegetable oil (not olive oil)**
- **8 cups mixed baby greens**
- **1 red pepper, cut crosswise in rounds**
- **½ white onion, cut crosswise in ½-inch rounds**
- **⅓ lb. Gorgonzola cheese, crumbled**
- **¼ cup chopped toasted walnuts**

Bill Davisson
Washington Hills Cellars
Kirkland, WA

Maine Lobster Salad with Citrus, Tomato and Extra-Virgin Olive Oil

Serves 4
Preparation Time:
20 Minutes (note marinating time)

- **1½ lbs. Maine lobster, poached, shelled**
- **1 pink grapefruit, peeled, segmented**
- **2 oranges, peeled, segmented**
- **1 lime, peeled, segmented**
- **1 tomato, peeled, seeded, julienned**
- **2 shallots, chopped**
- **1 garlic clove, chopped**
- **1 Tbsp. chives, chopped**
- **2 basil leaves, finely sliced**
- **3 Tbsps. extra-virgin olive oil**
- **Salt and pepper to taste**

Slice the lobster and set aside.

Mix all the ingredients together except for the lobster.

Marinate for about 15 minutes and place on a plate. Arrange the sliced lobster on top. Serve chilled.

Thierry Rautureau
Rover's
Seattle, Washington

Radicchio e Pancetta alla Griglia

Serves 6
Preparation Time:
30 Minutes

- **3 egg yolks**
- **3 Tbsps. Dijon mustard**
- **2 Tbsps. minced garlic**
- **¼ cup lemon juice**
- **¼ cup red wine vinegar**
- **2 cups olive oil**
- **¼ cup grated Parmesan cheese**
- **¾ cup to 1 cup fresh basil pesto**
- **Kosher salt and black pepper**
- **¼ cup goat cheese**
- **2 large heads of radicchio**
- **8 thin strips of pancetta or smoked bacon**
- **2 bamboo skewers, 10″ each**
- **¼ cup balsamic vinegar**
- **¼ cup extra-virgin olive oil**
- **Basil leaves for garnish**

To prepare the vinaigrette, combine the egg yolks, mustard, garlic, lemon juice, vinegar and a pinch of salt in a food processor for one minute. While still mixing on the highest speed, slowly drizzle the olive oil into the mixture, increasing the flow as the vinaigrette thickens.

Remove the vinaigrette to a medium-sized mixing bowl, then fold in the Parmesan cheese and the pesto. Salt and pepper to taste. Vinaigrette should be a deep green color. Ladle vinaigrette onto a serving plate and dot with goat cheese. Refrigerate until ready to serve.

Cut each head of radicchio into 4 equal pieces (cut at the root so that the pieces are held together). Wrap each piece of radicchio with the pancetta, then slide 4 pieces onto each bamboo skewer, making sure to skewer through the pancetta so that it does not unwrap from the radicchio.

Brush the radicchio with balsamic vinegar and extra-virgin olive oil. Grill the skewers over charcoal or wood barbecue, turning frequently. Cook until pancetta is golden brown and radicchio is wilted and hot throughout. Remove from heat.

Remove from skewer and arrange on plate on top of vinaigrette with the cores meeting at the center. Garnish center with the top leaves of a stalk of fresh basil. Serve immediately.

David Machado
Pazzo Ristorante
Portland, Oregon

☆

Wilted Spinach Salad with Smoked Duck and Bacon

Serves 4
Preparation Time:
30 Minutes

- **1 cup sugar**
- **¼ cup Worcestershire sauce**
- **¼ cup red wine vinegar**
- **2 Tbsps. dry English mustard**
- **1½ cups canola oil**
- **¼ cup bacon, cooked, diced**
- **¼ cup smoked duck, diced**
- **⅓ cup brandy**
- **1 lb. spinach, cleaned**

In a mixing bowl combine the sugar, Worcestershire sauce, red wine vinegar and mustard. Slowly drizzle in the canola oil while whisking. Set aside.

In a sauté pan, over medium heat, add the cooked bacon, smoked duck and brandy. Let brandy flame and sauce reduce.

Add the dressing and bring to a boil.

Place the spinach in a serving bowl and pour the sauce over the spinach. Toss the spinach until slightly wilted and serve.

Britt Unkerfer
Columbia Gorge Hotel
Hood River, Oregon

Seafood

Grilled Ahi in a Sesame Seed Crust with Wasabe Cream Sauce

Serves 4
Preparation Time:
30 Minutes

- **1 Tbsp. olive oil**
- **2 large shallots, minced**
- **1 large garlic clove, minced**
- **¼ cup Chardonnay**
- **1 tsp. wasabe paste**
- **⅔ cup heavy cream**
- **2 Tbsps. fish stock or water**
- **3 Tbsps. sesame oil, divided**
- **2 Tbsps. honey**
- **4 ahi tuna filets, 5 oz. each**
- **Sea salt and freshly ground pepper**
- **¼ cup sesame seeds, toasted**
- **1 Tbsp. fresh cilantro, chopped**

To prepare the wasabe cream sauce, heat the olive oil in a skillet over moderate heat. Add the shallots and cook until softened, about 4 minutes. Add the garlic and cook until fragrant, about 1 minute more. Increase the heat to medium-high and add the Chardonnay. Boil until the wine is reduced by half.

Stir in the wasabe paste, heavy cream and fish stock and bring to a simmer. Continue to simmer until the cream is slightly thickened. Remove from heat and keep warm.

In a small bowl, whisk together 2 Tbsps. sesame oil and the honey. Set aside.

To prepare the fish, brush the filets with the remaining 1 Tbsp. of the sesame oil and season with salt and pepper. Grill to desired doneness. After the steaks have been removed from the grill, brush their sides with the honey-oil mixture. Roll the steaks in the sesame seeds, coating only the sides, not the top or bottom.

Place the steaks on a warmed plate and spoon the wasabe cream sauce around the filet and finish by sprinkling with chopped cilantro.

Mike Caldwell
Flerchinger Vineyards
Hood River Valley, Oregon

Chilean Sea Bass with a Vine Ripened Yellow Tomato Coulis

To sauté the sea bass, season the filets with salt and pepper and sauté the fish in a very hot pan with 1 Tbsp. olive oil, until the fish is golden in color. Place in a 450° oven for about 5 minutes.

To prepare the sauce, heat a shallow pan with 1 Tbsp. olive oil. Sauté the diced vegetables until soft, then add the diced tomatoes. Add the white wine and let simmer for about 6 minutes. Purée the sauce and season to taste.

Season the sauce, pour on heated plates, covering the bottom of the plate. Place the sea bass on the sauce. Garnish with parsley leaves.

COOKING SECRET: This dish is also delicious if you choose to use fresh halibut, and accompanied with steamed baby vegetables and potatoes.

Serves 4
Preparation Time:
35 Minutes
Pre-heat oven to 450°

4 pieces Chilean sea bass
Salt and pepper
2 Tbsps. olive oil
½ stalk celery, diced
½ carrot, diced
½ onion, diced
1 garlic clove, peeled and diced
6 yellow tomatoes (or red if not available), diced
½ cup dry white wine
1 bunch Italian parsley, garnish

Markus Wieland
The Alabaster Restaurant
Vancouver, British Columbia

Provencial Prawns

Serves 4
Preparation Time:
30 Minutes

- **2 garlic cloves, sliced**
- **3 Tbsps. olive oil**
- **1 lb. prawns, peeled and cleaned**
- **12 medium mushrooms**
- **4 Roma tomatoes, blanched, peeled and diced**
- **½ cup dry white wine**
- **Juice from one lemon**
- **2 tsps. butter**
- **2 Tbsps. chopped parsley**
- **Salt and pepper to taste**

Sauté the garlic in olive oil till golden. Add the prawns and sauté one minute on each side at medium heat. Add the mushrooms and sauté untill translucent.

Add the tomatoes and cook while stirring for one minute. Add the wine and lemon juice. Simmer for a minute.

Stir in the butter over low heat. Add the parsley and season to taste with salt and pepper.

COOKING SECRET: This dish is delicious alone or served over rice.

Carmine Smeraldo
Il Terrazzo Carmine
Seattle, Washington

Halibut and Fresh Chanterelles Simmered in Vietnamese-Style Caramel Sauce

Prepare the sauce by placing the sugar and lemon juice in a heavy saucepan over medium heat until the sugar has melted and takes on a golden brown color. While the sugar is melting, occasionally brush the sides of the saucepan with a pastry brush dipped in cold water to help prevent crystallization. Add the fish sauce, stirring occasionally. Remove the sauce from the heat and add the shallots and black pepper. This step can be done up to a week in advance.

Prepare the mushrooms by removing any debris with damp paper towels. Halve or quarter the large mushrooms; otherwise leave them whole to show off their lovely shape.

Place the fish, the sauce and the mushrooms in a skillet large enough to hold everything without crowding. Heat slowly to a gentle simmer. Gently turn the fish portions over, cover the pan, and cook for another 5 minutes.

Gently fold the orange zest into the rice after cooking.

To serve, place a mound of cooked rice in the center of 6 dinner plates. Boil the snow peas for 1 minute and divide amongst the 6 plates, placing them atop the pile of rice. Place a fish portion on top of the snow peas, distribute the mushrooms and spoon about ¼ cup sauce over the fish. Sprinkle with chives and serve.

COOKING SECRET: Halibut season, which we look forward to all winter, was in its last week, and word was out that chanterelles were fading as well. Marrying the two was my way of hoping the season could last just a little longer. Of course, it didn't work, but we did stumble onto a unique and satisfying combination of flavors.

Serves 6
Preparation Time:
45 Minutes

- **4 cups granulated sugar**
- **2 tsps. lemon juice**
- **1 bottle (17 oz.) good quality nouc nam (Vietnamese fish sauce)**
- **6 large shallots, thinly sliced**
- **1 Tbsp. ground black pepper**
- **1 lb. fresh chanterelles**
- **2¼ lbs. fresh halibut filet, divided into 6 portions**
- **½ lb. snow peas, strings removed, julienned**
- **3 cups prepared rice (preferably jasmine or basmati)**
- **Zest of 1 orange**
- **1 cup snow peas**
- **1 small bunch chives, cut into ⅛ inch lengths**

John Zenger
River Place Hotel
Portland, Oregon

☆

Good Night Salmon

Serves 4
Preparation Time:
25 Minutes (Note Marinating Time)

- **4 salmon filets**
- **4 Tbsps. miso paste**
- **2 Tbsps. Mirin (Japanese cooking wine)**
- **1 Tbsp. sake**
- **1 Tbsp. sesame oil**
- **1 Tbsp. sugar**
- **Dash of ground red chile pepper**
- **1 Tbsp. freshly ground ginger**
- **½ cup green onions, chopped, garnish**
- **½ cup shiitake mushrooms, chopped, garnish**

Rinse salmon and cut into bite-sized pieces. Set aside.

In a mixing bowl, combine the miso paste, Mirin, sake, sesame oil, sugar, chile pepper and ground ginger to create a marinade.

Place the salmon portions in the marinade overnight, refrigerated.

Bake salmon at 350° degrees for 12 to 15 minutes.

Before serving, garnish with green onions and shiitake mushrooms.

Hidekazu Tojo
Tojo's Restaurant
Vancouver, British Columbia

Salmon in a Crispy Skin Crust with Pancetta, Honey, and Tamari Soy Sauce

Serves 8
Preparation Time:
25 Minutes

- **8 salmon filets, with skin on, 6 oz. each**
- **Salt and pepper to taste**
- **1 Tbsp. virgin olive oil**
- **1½ cups white wine**
- **1 Tbsp. garlic, chopped**
- **2 Tbsps. honey**
- **2 Tbsps. tamari soy sauce**
- **2½ cups fish stock or clam juice**
- **3⅓ cups whipping cream**
- **1½ Tbsps. pancetta, cooked, diced**

Season the salmon with salt and freshly ground pepper.

Heat the olive oil in a pan and sauté the salmon on one side for 5 minutes or until lightly brown. Turn the fish over and cook for another 3 to 5 minutes depending on the thickness. The salmon tastes best if cooked medium-rare to medium.

Add the white wine and garlic and reduce by two-thirds. Add the honey, tamari, and fish stock or clam juice and reduce by one-third. Add the cream and the pancetta and reduce by one-third.

Drizzle the sauce over the salmon before serving.

Nicolas Adam
L'Auberge
Portland, Oregon

☆

Maple & Bourbon Marinated Pacific Home Smoked Salmon with Chili & Chive Infused Oil

Serves 6
Preparation Time:
30 Minutes (Note Marinating Time)

- **6 fresh salmon filets, 6 oz. each**
- **2 oz. Wild Turkey Bourbon**
- **⅓ cup Canadian maple syrup**
- **Cherry or alderwood chips for smoking**
- **1 Tbsp. canola oil**

Chili & Chive Infused Oil
- **4 Tbsps. fresh shallots**
- **2 Tbsps. fresh garlic, chopped**
- **1 small pinch dried chile peppers**
- **¾ cup extra-virgin olive oil**
- **4 Tbsps. fresh chives, (approximately 1 bunch)**
- **Salt and pepper to taste**

Marinate the salmon in bourbon and maple syrup for 6 to 8 hours. After the salmon has marinated, dry smoke the fish for 7 to10 minutes using cherry and alderwood chips.

In a smoking hot sauté pan, 1 Tbsp. oil. Sear the salmon on both sides. Bake for 5 to 6 minutes in a 375° oven. For best results, serve salmon medium-rare.

Chili & Chive Infused Oil

In a heavy-bottomed, sauté pan over medium heat, sauté the shallots for 2 minutes. Add the garlic and chili peppers and sauté for 1 minute. Add the olive oil and let stand to cool. When at room temperature, blend in the chives, season with salt and pepper and strain with cheesecloth.

COOKING SECRET: Serve the salmon with fresh vegetables and steamed minted potatoes. Drizzle with the chive and chili infused oil.

Daryle Ryo Nagata
Waterfront Centre Hotel
Vancouver, British Columbia

Oven-Roasted Salmon with a Hazelnut Crust and Tomato Vinaigrette with Herbed Morel Barley

In a 350° oven, roast the hazelnuts on a cookie sheet for approximately 10 to 12 minutes or until the skins crack. Remove from the oven while still warm. Rub the hazelnuts together, removing as much of the bitter, dark skin as possible. In a food processor fitted with a metal blade, purée the nuts until smooth. Transfer to a shallow dish.

In a bowl, make an egg wash by whisking together the egg yolk and water.

Dredge the salmon filets with seasoned flour. Dip the top side of each filet in the egg wash and coat generously with the ground hazelnuts. Lightly pat down the coating. Place in the refrigerator for 20 minutes prior to cooking.

In a sauté pan, heat the oil and gently place the salmon, crust side down. Agitate the pan slightly so the fish will not stick to the pan. Cook for approximately 2 minutes and turn the fish over. Transfer to a 350° oven and finish to desired doneness.

COOKING SECRET: It is very important to start with lightly toasted hazelnuts, beige in color. The crust takes on more color after it has been oven-roasted and the nuts have a tendency to get bitter.

Monique Barbeau
Fullers
Seattle, Washington

Serves 6
Preparation Time:
30 Minutes (Note Refrigeration Time)
Pre-heat oven to 350°

¾ cup hazelnuts
1 egg yolk
2 Tbsps. water
6 salmon filets, 5 oz. each
¼ cup flour, seasoned with salt and pepper
2 to 3 Tbsps. oil

Onion Tomato Vinaigrette

Preparation Time:
30 Minutes

- **6 onions, Walla Walla preferably; reserve 2, finely diced**
- **Olive oil, to coat onions**
- **¾ cup sherry vinegar**
- **¼ cup sun-dried tomatoes**
- **1 cup olive oil**
- **4 tomatoes, peeled, deseeded, chopped**
- **Juice of 1 lemon, optional**
- **Salt and pepper to taste**

Morel Barley
Preparation Time:
45 Minutes
Pre-heat oven to 350°

- **4 Tbsps. oil**
- **½ cup onion, diced**
- **1 cup barley**
- **2 to 2½ cups chicken stock**
- **1 large shallot, minced**
- **2 cups morel mushrooms, cleaned, quartered lengthwise**
- **¾ cup Pinot Noir wine**
- **1 tsp. salt and pepper**
- **¼ cup fresh herbs, chopped**

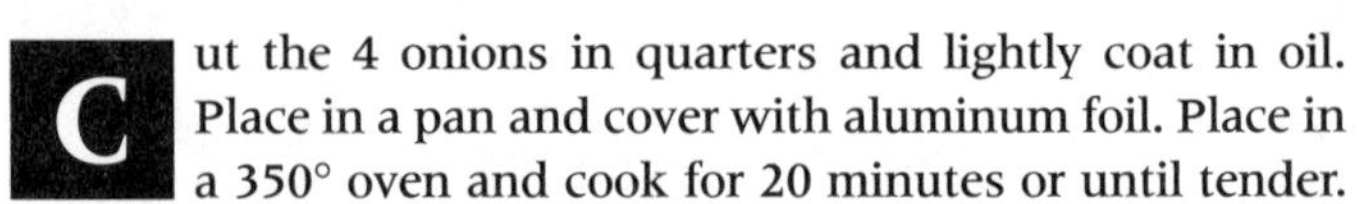

Cut the 4 onions in quarters and lightly coat in oil. Place in a pan and cover with aluminum foil. Place in a 350° oven and cook for 20 minutes or until tender.

In a blender, purée the cooked onions with the vinegar until smooth. Add the sun-dried tomatoes and with the machine still running slowly pour in the oil. Transfer liquid to a bowl and mix in diced onion and fresh chopped tomato. Add lemon juice if necessary and season with salt and pepper.

Morel Barley

This vinaigrette can be served at room temperature or heated slightly.

In a medium saucepan heat 2 Tbsps. oil and gently sweat the onions until soft and translucent. Add the barley and stir until well coated. Add the chicken stock and bring to a boil. Cover with a tight-fitting lid and transfer to a 350° oven. Let cook for approximately 30 minutes.

In a sauté pan over medium-high heat sauté the minced shallots in 2 Tbsps. oil. Add the morels and cook for 3 minutes, stirring often. Add the red wine and let reduce until dry.

Remove the barley from the oven and stir in the cooked morels. Toss in the fresh herbs and season with salt and pepper.

To assemble this dish, make a mound with the barley in the center of the plate, using circle molds if available. Spoon the vinaigrette around the perimeter. Place the hazelnut salmon on top.

Monique Barbeau
Fullers
Seattle, Washington

Sautéed Salmon with Red Pepper Coulis and Fennel Slaw

Serves 4
Preparation Time:
35 Minutes
Pre-heat oven to 375°

- **4 salmon filets, 5 oz. each**
- **2 red bell peppers**
- **1 fennel bulb**
- **2 Tbsps. butter**
- **3 shallots, thinly sliced**
- **4 mushrooms, thinly sliced**
- **1 sprig fresh thyme**
- **6 to 8 parsley stems**
- **1 tsp. black pepper**
- **1 cup sherry vinegar**
- **2 cups heavy cream**
- **1 bunch chives, finely chopped**
- **2 Tbsps. olive oil**
- **Salt to taste**

Rinse salmon filets, set aside.

Roast peppers in a 375° oven until soft. While hot, place in a bowl covered with plastic until skin is loosened. Peel, seed, and set aside. Thinly shave fennel. Place in ice water, refrigerate, and set aside.

In a thick-bottomed pot, melt the butter and add shallots, mushrooms, thyme, parsley, and black pepper. Sweat slowly, then add the sherry vinegar and reduce to ¼ cup.

Add the heavy cream and reduce slowly to sauce consistency.

Strain sauce into a blender, add the red peppers, and blend thoroughly. Keep sauce warm and reserve.

Strain fennel, dry, and toss in olive oil and chives.

Sauté the salmon in a nonstick pan to desired tenderness.

To serve, pour the sauce into the center of a warm plate and place the salmon in the middle. Top with the crispy fennel slaw. Garnish with chopped chives.

Britt Unkerfer
Columbia Gorge Hotel
Hood River, Oregon

Thai Curry Sea Scallops

Serves 4
Preparation Time:
15 Minutes

- **2 Tbsps. peanut oil**
- **20 large sea scallops**
- **3 Tbsps. curry paste**
- **⅔ cup chicken stock**
- **½ cup coconut milk**

Pour the peanut oil in a large nonstick skillet. Heat to smoking. Remove from flame and quickly add the scallops to the pan, one by one. Return to flame and sear the scallops on one side, then the other. This process should take approximately 4 to 5 minutes. The scallops will be medium rare. Remove the scallops to a warm platter and discard excess grease from pan.

Add the curry paste and sauté briefly.

Add the chicken stock and reduce by half.

Add the coconut milk and continue to simmer until the sauce is thick enough to coat a spoon.

To serve, pour the sauce over scallops.

COOKING SECRET: Curry pastes are available in many food markets, particularly Asian specialty stores.

Christine Keff
Flying Fish
Seattle, Washington

☆

Sunlight Beach Marinated Shrimp

Peel, clean and cook shrimp until pink; run under cold water, set aside to cool.

In a large mixing bowl combine the olive oil, lemon juice, parsley, salt and garlic. Add the shrimp and marinate for 6 to 8 hours or longer.

COOKING SECRET: This recipe can be adapted for chicken, using 2 boneless chicken breasts, sliced into strips. Marinate overnight, then stir fry or grill.

Serves 4
Prep Time: 20 minutes
(Note Marinating Time)

1½ lbs. shrimp
1 cup olive oil
2 Tbsps. lemon juice
2 Tbsps. parley, chopped
½ tsp. salt
3 garlic cloves, minced

Linda Drew-Walsh
Home by the Sea/French Rd. Farm
Clinton, Washington

Chicken Breast with Fresh Peaches and Hazelnut Breading

Chicken Breasts in Wine Sauce

Chicken Breasts Stuffed with Hazelnuts in Champagne Sauce

Glazed Chicken and Pea Pods

Poulet au Feu D'Enfer

Roast Gingered Turkey Breast and Couscous with Raisins and Red Peppers

Chicken Breast with Fresh Peaches and Hazelnut Breading

Slowly poach peaches in wine, sugar and cinnamon until tender. Strain peaches from sauce. Reduce sauce until thickened. Fold peaches back into the sauce. Set aside.

In a large mixing bowl, combine the hazelnuts, crackermeal, salt and pepper.

Dredge the boneless, skinless chicken breasts in flour, then egg wash and then the hazelnut breading. Press breading firmly into the chicken.

Sauté lightly in vegetable oil, then bake at 350° for 30 minutes or until the chicken is done.

Before serving, top with the fresh peach sauce.

COOKING SECRET: This recipe works equally well with fresh pears. Add ¼ cup apple juice concentrate to the sauce before cooking.

Serves 4
Preparation Time:
One Hour
Pre-heat oven to 350°

- **4 ripe peaches, sliced**
- **2 cups white wine**
- **¼ cup sugar**
- **2 tsps. cinnamon**
- **1½ cups hazelnuts, finely ground**
- **1 cup crackermeal**
- **Salt and pepper to taste**
- **½ cup flour**
- **4 half chicken breasts, boned and skinned**
- **3 eggs, beaten**
- **Vegetable oil**

Jerry and Linda Evans
Jacksonville Inn Dinner House
Jacksonville, Oregon

Chicken Breasts in Wine Sauce

Serves 4
Preparation Time: 1½ Hours
Cooking Time: One Hour
Pre-heat oven to 350°

- **2 lbs. chicken breasts, halved**
- **Salt and pepper to taste**
- **Flour to dust chicken and thicken sauce**
- **Cooking oil**
- **1 cup onion, diced**
- **1¼ cups chicken stock**
- **1 cup Sauvignon Blanc wine**
- **5 to 6 drops Tabasco sauce**
- **½ tsp. sugar**

Season the chicken to taste with salt and pepper and coat with flour. Heat oil in heavy frying pan. Brown chicken and place in an oven pan. Drain all but 2 or 3 tsps. of oil from the frying pan.

Add the onion, cook 1 minute, add the stock, wine, Tabasco and sugar. Stir until warm, then whisk in 1 tsp. flour.

Pour over chicken and bake in oven at 350° for 1 hour.

Scott Pontin
Pontin Del Roza Winery
Prosser, Washington

Chicken Breasts Stuffed with Hazelnuts in Champagne Sauce

In a small mixing bowl, blend the cream cheese, hazelnuts and scallions. With the tip of a sharp boning knife, cut a small pocket lengthwise in the side of each chicken breast. Divide the stuffing evenly and press into the pockets of the chicken breasts. Melt 4 Tbsps. of the butter and brush the bottom of the baking dish, and the tops of the chicken breasts. Season the breasts lightly with salt and pepper. Place the breasts in the baking dish in a single layer, cover with a lid or foil, and bake for 12 minutes. Turn the breasts and cook approximately 8 to 10 minutes more or until done.

In a small saucepan, combine the champagne, demi-glace, shallots and lemon juice, and reduce over high heat until only about ½ remains. Add the cream and reduce the liquid volume again by half. Reduce the heat and gently whisk in the remaining butter in small pieces until fully incorporated.

Arrange the chicken breasts on a serving plate and nap with champagne sauce. Garnish with toasted hazelnuts, parsley sprigs and lemon wedges.

Michael Donovan and David Taub
Chateaulin Restaurant
Ashland, Oregon

Serves 4
Preparation Time:
45 Minutes
Preheat oven to 400°

- **½ lb. cream cheese**
- **½ cup roasted hazelnuts, skins removed, coarsely chopped**
- **2 scallions, minced**
- **8 fresh chicken breasts, boneless, skinless, about 4 oz. each**
- **½ cup (1 stick) unsalted butter**
- **Salt and white pepper**
- **¾ cup dry sparkling wine or French champagne**
- **¾ cup demi-glace (reduced brown stock)**
- **2 Tbsps. shallots, chopped**
- **Juice of 1 lemon**
- **½ cup heavy cream**
- **Toasted hazelnuts, garnish**
- **Parsley, garnish**
- **Lemon wedges, garnish**

Glazed Chicken and Pea Pods

Serves 4
Preparation Time:
30 Minutes

- **11 oz. can mandarin oranges**
- **2 Tbsps. Loganberry wine**
- **4 Tbsps. soy sauce**
- **1 Tbsp. cornstarch**
- **¼ tsp. ginger, ground**
- **⅛ tsp. aniseed, crushed**
- **Dash ground red pepper**
- **Dash ground cloves**
- **2½ to 3 lb. broiler-fryer chicken, cut up**
- **1 cup frozen pea pods**
- **Walnut halves**

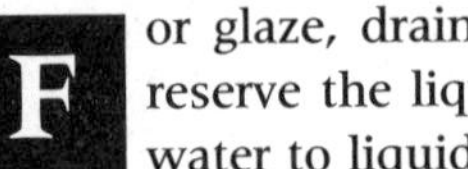

For glaze, drain the oranges into a 2 cup measure: reserve the liquid. Set fruit aside. If necessary, add water to liquid to equal ½ cup. Add the Loganberry wine, 2 Tbsps. soy sauce, cornstarch, ginger, aniseed, red pepper, and cloves. Microwave uncovered on high power for 3 to 5 minutes or until thickened and bubbly, stirring every minute until slightly thickened, then every 30 seconds.

In a 12″×7½″ baking dish, arrange chicken pieces skin side down, with meaty portions toward edges. Brush with soy sauce. Cover with wax paper. Cook in microwave on high for 5 minutes. Give dish a half turn, turn pieces skin side up, and rearrange, putting cooked portions toward center. Brush with soy sauce. Cook covered for 5 minutes and drain.

Meanwhile, run cold water over frozen pea pods in a colander until separated. Add pea pods, walnuts and orange sections to chicken. Pour glaze over all. Cover with wax paper. Cook on high 3 to 5 minutes more or until chicken and pea pods are done.

Peggy and Edwin Paterson
Hoodsport Winery
Hoodsport, Washington

☆

Poulet au Feu D'Enfer

In a large skillet, brown the chicken in oil over high heat. Discard excess oil and stir in the minced garlic, cooking for five to ten seconds. Do not allow it to brown. Add the white wine and red wine vinegar.

Brush each chicken piece with tomato paste. Add the chicken to wine mixture and bring to a boil, cooking uncovered until the liquid is reduced by one-fourth.

Stir in the stock and tarragon. Return to boiling; cover and simmer on low heat for 20 to 30 minutes or until the chicken is tender.

With a slotted spoon, remove the chicken to a serving platter. Keep warm.

Over high heat, bring the sauce to a boil, cooking uncovered until the volume is reduced to one-half cup. Season to taste with salt and pepper. Whisk in the butter and parsley. Spoon the sauce over the chicken and serve.

James Beals
Heron Haus
Portland, Oregon

Serves 4
Preparation Time: One Hour

4 chicken legs with thighs
2 Tbsps. vegetable oil
1 tsp. garlic, minced
¼ cup dry white wine
¾ cup red wine vinegar
1 Tbsp. tomato paste
½ cup chicken stock
½ tsp. dried tarragon
Salt and freshly ground pepper to taste
1 Tbsp. unsalted butter
1 tsp. parsley, minced

Roast Gingered Turkey Breast and Couscous with Raisins and Red Peppers

Serves 4
Preparation Time:
45 Minutes
Pre-heat oven to 350°

- **3 cloves garlic, finely chopped**
- **¾ tsp. ground cinnamon**
- **2 Tbsps. fresh ginger, peeled, grated**
- **¼ cup unsalted chicken stock**
- **1 tsp. dark sesame oil**
- **1 Tbsp. low-sodium soy sauce**
- **1½ lbs. turkey breast**
- **2 tsps. safflower oil**

Couscous with Raisins and Red Peppers

- **1 tsp. olive oil**
- **⅓ cup onions, finely chopped**
- **½ cup sweet red pepper, cubed**
- **1¼ cup boiling water**
- **⅓ cup raisins (golden raisins are preferable)**
- **⅛ tsp. ground cinnamon**
- **¼ tsp. ground cumin**
- **½ tsp. grated orange rind**
- **Salt and freshly ground pepper to taste**
- **1 cup quick-cooking couscous**
- **1 Tbsp. unsalted butter**

To make the marinade, combine the garlic, cinnamon, ginger, stock, sesame oil and soy sauce in a shallow bowl just large enough to hold the turkey breast.

Pierce the breast with several ½-inch deep slits in the thick part of the meat. Put the turkey in the bowl with the marinade and turn it to coat. Cover and refrigerate for 8 to 24 hours, turning occasionally. (I have also done this dish in a hurry and only marinated for a few minutes).

Allow the turkey to come to room temperature and remove from the marinade. Reserve the marinade.

Heat the safflower oil in a heavy-bottomed, oven-proof skillet over medium-high heat. Sauté the turkey until golden brown on one side, about 4 minutes, and turn. Baste with the accumulated juices and cook another 4 minutes. Remove from heat and pour the reserved marinade over the turkey. Put the skillet in the oven and roast the turkey until it feels firm but springy to the touch, about 15 to 20 minutes. Baste once during cooking. When done, let the turkey cool for 5 minutes, then cut into ¼-inch slices.

Couscous with Raisins and Red Peppers

In a sauce pan with a tight lid, heat the olive oil. Add the onions and red peppers and cook, stirring until wilted. Do not brown. Add the water, raisins, cinnamon, cumin, orange rind, salt and pepper. Bring to a boil. Remove the mixture from the heat; add the couscous and stir well. Cover and let stand for 5 minutes. Uncover, add butter and fluff well with a fork.

Serve turkey slices with the couscous on the side.

Tom and Wendy Kreutner
Autumn Wind Vineyard
Newberg, Oregon

☆

Breast of Duck with Sweet Plums and Pancetta-Wrapped Potatoes

Duck Breast with Fresh Oregon Currants

Duck Breast with Wild Mushrooms and Armagnac Sauce

Portobello and Game Brochettes

Roast Quail with Prosciutto

Sautéed Rabbit with Rhubarb and Hazelnut Sauce

Herb Crusted Fallow Venison Loin

Breast of Duck with Sweet Plums and Pancetta-Wrapped Potatoes

Serves 4
Preparation Time: 45 Minutes
Cooking Time: 40 Minutes
Pre-heat oven to 350°

- **4 russet potatoes, peeled, cut in half lengthwise, pared down to a uniform size**
- **8 thin slices of pancetta or bacon**
- **8 ripe plums**
- **¼ cup balsamic vinegar**
- **2 Tbsps. olive oil**
- **1 Tbsp. cracked black pepper**
- **1 Tbsp. cracked fennel seeds**
- **4 duck breasts**
- **Salt and pepper**
- **1 Tbsp. butter**
- **½ lb. fresh spinach leaves**

Place the potatoes in a saucepan, cover with water and boil until soft, about 15 minutes. Drain and cool. When potatoes are cool, wrap each piece in a slice of the pancetta or bacon and place on a baking sheet.

Cut the plums in half and remove the seeds. Place plums in a bowl and toss with vinegar, olive oil, black pepper and fennel seeds. Let stand for at least 15 minutes. Place plums on baking sheet with potatoes.

Trim duck breasts of any excess fat and score the fat with a knife, being careful not to pierce the skin.

Heat a large sauté pan, season the duck breasts with salt and pepper and place fat side down in pan. Begin to render fat off the duck and discard as fat accumulates in pan.

Place plums and pancetta-wrapped potatoes in a 350° oven to bake for 20 minutes.

When ducks are rendered, about 8 minutes, turn over to flesh side and place in oven for 5 minutes or until medium rare.

Melt butter in sauté pan and begin to wilt spinach. Season with salt and pepper.

To finish, arrange spinach, potatoes and plums on plates. Slice duck breasts against the grain and place on plates.

Cory Schreiber
Wildwood Restaurant
Portland, Oregon

☆

Duck Breast with Fresh Oregon Currants

Using a sharp knife, score the skin of the duck breasts in a diamond pattern, 3 cuts in each direction. The cuts should go through the skin but not into the meat. Leave skin on the breasts. Season both sides with salt and pepper.

Heat peanut oil in sauté pan large enough to hold breasts comfortably. Skin side down, cook slowly for 8 minutes (rare) to 12 minutes (medium rare), carefully pouring off fat as it gathers in pan but leave enough duck fat in the pan to cook other side of breasts. Turn breasts over and cook for 5 minutes. Remove breasts from pan and be sure to keep duck warm.

Pour off all fat from pan and deglaze by adding duck stock. Reduce duck stock by half over medium heat and add Creme de Cassis. Lower heat and whisk butter into liquid. Strain liquid through fine-mesh sieve into small sauce pan. Add currants to warm.

Slice duck breasts with sharp serrated knife. Arrange duck in fan shape on plate and spoon sauce over duck.

Serves 2
Preparation Time: 3 Hours

- **1 medium sized duck, breasts and legs removed (Save carcass for stock. You will not need the legs for this dish so reserve them in the freezer for future recipes)**
- **¼ cup fresh red currants**
- **¼ cup fresh black currants**
- **1 Tbsp. peanut oil**
- **2 Tbsps. Creme de Cassis**
- **1½ cup duck stock (recipe to follow)**
- **2 Tbsp. butter**
- **Salt & pepper to taste**

Duck Stock

In a pot large enough to hold duck carcass, heat oil on high until hot but not smoking. Add carcass and brown on all sides. Add vegetables and brown 5 minutes more. Add wine and stock and bring to a simmer. Once simmering, lower heat and cook for 2 hours.

Strain through cheesecloth and de-fat stock.

Duck Stock
(Yields 2½–3 cups)

- **1 Tbsp. oil**
- **1 duck carcass**
- **1 lb. of vegetables (onions, carrots, celery)**
- **2 cups red wine**
- **1 qt. rich stock (veal or chicken)**

Dave Marth
3 Doors Down
Portland, Oregon

☆

Duck Breast with Wild Mushrooms and Armagnac Sauce

Serves 4
Preparation Time:
One Hour
Pre-heat oven to 400°

4 Tbsps. butter
Bones from 1 duck
½ onion, diced
1 carrot, diced
1 celery stalk, diced
1 cup + 2 Tbsps. Armagnac
3 cups veal stock
2 Tbsps. walnut oil
4 porcini mushrooms, diced
3 shallots, chopped
½ tsp. garlic, chopped
1 Tbsp. parsley, chopped
8 chanterelle mushrooms
2 duck breasts, about 9 oz. each

In a sauce pot, cook 2 Tbsps. butter until it is hazelnut-colored, then add the bones. Bring the bones to a sear and add all the vegetables, cooking them until they are browned. Add one cup of Armagnac, being careful not to create a flame, reduce it to one-fourth, and add the veal stock. Reduce the stock by half, then strain through a fine-mesh strainer. Return sauce to the fire and bring to a boil. Incorporate 2 Tbsps. butter and finish with 2 Tbsps. of Armagnac. Season to taste and keep hot until served.

In a hot skillet, add the walnut oil and the porcini mushrooms. Cook until they have a nice blond color, then add half of the shallots and half of the garlic. Cook for a few minutes and finish with the parsley. Set aside. Repeat with the chantrelles and the rest of the shallots and garlic. Set aside. The porcini and chanterelles will be mixed together and served alongside the duck.

In a hot skillet, sear the duck breasts on the skin side, then flip them and sear on the other side. Turn the breasts back onto the skin side and place in a 400° oven for a few minutes. Once cooked, let the meat rest for at least four minutes. Slice the duck breast and serve with the mushrooms on the side and the sauce on top.

Thierry Rautureau
Rover's
Seattle, Washington

☆

Portobello and Game Brochettes

Alternate the game and mushrooms on skewers, 3 pieces each per skewer. Set aside.

Purée the garlic, soy sauce, black bean sauce and pepper in a food processor. Brush on the brochettes 20 minutes before cooking.

Reduce the Pinot Noir and shallots over medium heat until almost dry. Swirl in the butter and parsley.

Broil the marinated brochettes approximately 3 minutes on each side, or until done.

COOKING SECRET: Any type of game may be used (elk, venison, quail, or duck), but chicken, beef and lamb work just as well. Any variety of mushroom may be used, but consider button mushrooms, morels, chanterelle, cremini, or shiitakes.

Joe Campell
Elk Cove Vineyards
Gaston, Oregon

Serves 4
Preparation Time: 45 Minutes
Cooking Time: 30 Minutes

- **6 oz. rabbit, cut in ¾-inch cubes**
- **6 oz. pheasant, cut in ¾-inch cubes**
- **3 portobello mushrooms, cut in 1-inch pieces**
- **1 tsp. garlic**
- **3 Tbsps. soy sauce**
- **1 Tbsp. black bean sauce**
- **½ tsp. pepper**
- **2 cups Pinot Noir**
- **2 Tbsps. shallots**
- **¼ cup butter**
- **1 Tbsp. parsley, chopped**

Roast Quail with Prosciutto

Serves 2
Preparation Time:
One Hour
Pre-heat oven to 400°

- **4 large quails**
- **4 thin slices of Parma prosciutto**
- **1 cup cremini mushrooms, sliced**
- **2 Tbsps. unsalted butter**
- **Fresh sage**
- **¼ cup brandy**
- **¾ cup veal stock**

Lightly dust the quails with flour to avoid sticking. Brown the quails over medium heat. Remove from the saucepan and wrap with prosciutto. Place in a 400° oven for 15 minutes or until cooked.

In a saucepan with drippings, add the mushrooms, butter and sage until mushrooms are tender. Flame with the brandy. Add the veal stock and reduce by half.

Place quail on plate with sauce. Serve immediately.

Donald Alcorn and Andrew Elarth
Al Boccalino Ristorante
Seattle, Washington

Sautéed Rabbit with Rhubarb and Hazelnut Sauce

Serves 4
Preparation Time:
45 Minutes

- 2 rabbits
- ¼ cup (½ stick) butter
- Salt and pepper to taste
- 1¾ cup port wine
- 1 lb. rhubarb, cut into small pieces
- 1 cup hazelnuts, blanched, toasted
- 3 cups stock
- 1½ cups port
- ¾ cup cognac

Remove the legs and filets from the rabbits. Remove sinews from the filets. Bone the legs by first taking out the hip bone, then the kneecap. Cut around the thigh bone from each end to detach it and pull it out of the leg meat, so that the meat is intact. Do not open the leg from the side.

Brown the rabbit in a sauté pan in butter for about 5 minutes for the filets and 10 minutes for the legs. The legs are done when the centers start to turn opaque. Keep the rabbit in a warm oven for 5 minutes. Salt and pepper to taste. Deglaze the pan with ¼ cup port. Cover and finish cooking rabbit over low heat or in a hot oven for 15 minutes.

In a non-aluminum sauce pan, cook the rhubarb, hazelnuts, stock, 1½ cups port and the cognac until the rhubarb is soft and has reduced by ⅔. Adjust seasonings to taste.

Serve the duck over a pool of the rhubarb hazelnut sauce.

Bruce Naftaly
Le Gourmand
Seattle, Washington

☆

Herb-Crusted Fallow Venison Loin with Salsify Purée and Huckleberry Mint Sauce

Serves 4
Preparation Time:
One Hour

- **4 venison loins, cleaned, 4 oz. each**
- **1 tsp. rosemary, chopped**
- **1 tsp. thyme, chopped**
- **Black pepper to taste**
- **1 lb. salsify (oyster plant), peeled**
- **¼ cup milk**
- **1 Tbsp. unsalted butter**
- **1 cup port**
- **½ cup fresh or frozen huckleberries**
- **2 cups venison or beef demi-glace**
- **1 Tbsp. fresh mint, chopped**

Coat the venison loins with the herbs and pepper, then pan-sear in a hot pan until brown on all sides. Remove from the pan and reserve until ready to serve.

Place the peeled salsify in a pot with milk and bring to a slow boil. Cook until tender, then remove from the pot and process in a food processor, adding 1 Tbsp. butter and some of the cooking milk. Process until smooth and season with salt and pepper to taste.

If salsify is not available, you can substitute potatoes, parsnips, celery root or sweet potatoes. Reserve the salsify until ready to serve.

Place the port in a saucepan and reduce it by two-thirds. Add the huckleberries and demi-glace and bring to a slow simmer. Add the mint and 1 tsp. butter, season with salt and pepper.

To serve, place a mound of salsify purée in the middle of each plate. Ladle the huckleberry mint sauce around the purée. Slice each loin of venison and fan around the purée.

Dean C. Ecker
The Salish Lodge at Snoqualmie Falls
Snoqualmie, WA

☆

Meat

Au Vin Rouge

Marinated Roast Beef

Grilled Leg of Lamb with Pinot Noir

Lamb Kebobs

Marinated Rack of Lamb with Minted Jus

Pacific Rim Lamb

Saddle of Lamb with Tarragon Mustard Sauce

Spit-Roasted Herb-Rubbed Leg of Lamb with Mint & Walnut Pesto Glaze

Stuffed Lamb Chops

Pork Tenderloin with Cabernet Port Sauce

Pork Tenderloin Stuffed with Wild Mushrooms

Grilled Stuffed Pork Chop

Roasted Loin of Pork with Pears and Vin Santo

Roasted Pork Tenderloin with a Rhubarb Mustard Puree

Great Gravy Pot Roast

Roast Prime Rib with Cabernet Sauce

Baked Ribs in Barbecue Sauce

Crock Pot Cabernet Roast

Veal and Prawn Involtini

Natural Veal Medallions

Au Vin Rouge

Serves 6
Preparation Time:
3½ Hours
Cooking Time: 3½—4 Hours
Pre-heat oven to 325°

8 to 10 lb. beef rib roast
4 Tbsps. butter, divided
⅓ cup carrot, chopped
⅓ cup onion, chopped
⅓ cup celery, chopped
2¼ cups Pinot Noir
1 clove garlic, crushed
3¼ cups beef broth
2 Tbsps. cornstarch
½ cup button mushrooms

Season the roast before cooking if desired. Place roast on rack in open pan in 325° oven. Then lower to 130° and roast for 3½ to 4 hours, depending on taste. Remove from oven and cover with foil. Let rest 20 minutes before carving.

Melt 1 Tbsp. butter in a saucepan. Add the vegetables and sauté. Add the Pinot Noir and cook until reduced by half. Add the garlic and beef broth and simmer 12 to 15 minutes.

Mix the cornstarch with 3 Tbsps. butter, stir until melted. Strain sauce. Add the mushrooms and heat through.

Ladle the sauce over the sliced beef.

Marj Vuylsteke
Oak Knoll Winery, Inc.
Hillsboro, Oregon

Marinated Roast Beef

Combine all the ingredients in a large, deep bowl; add the meat last.

Marinate for 24 hours, turning and stabbing the meat several times with a fork to allow the marinade to penetrate.

Place the meat in a rack in a roasting pan, baste with the marinade and roast at 425° for 3½ hours for rare meat. For medium steak, roast at 425° for 1 hour, then cover and reduce heat to 300°. Continue to cook for 4 hours basting periodically.

Peggy and Edwin Paterson
Hoodsport Winery
Hoodsport, Washington

Serves 6
Preparation Time:
15 Minutes (Note Marinating Time)
Cooking Time: 3½—4 Hours

- **2 cups Hoodsport Island Belle wine (or any red wine)**
- **2 cloves garlic, crushed**
- **¼ cup lemon juice**
- **1 tsp. ground pepper**
- **1 tsp. dry mustard**
- **1 cup salad oil**
- **1½ tsp. salt**
- **2 bay leaves**
- **1 tsp. oregano**
- **1 tsp. basil**
- **1 tsp. thyme**
- **8 to 10 lb. top round steak, cut and tied**

☆

Grilled Leg of Lamb with Pinot Noir

Serves 8
Preparation Time:
45 Minutes (note marinating time)

- **6 lbs. lamb leg, boned, butterflied**
- **1 cup Pinot Noir**
- **1 cup pomegranate juice, unsweetened**
- **2 large onions**
- **1 large lemon, unpeeled**
- **8 cloves garlic, peeled**
- **1 Tbsp. black peppercorns, ground**
- **1 Tbsp. tarragon leaves, dried**
- **1 tsp. sea salt**

Ask the butcher to butterfly and thoroughly trim a leg of lamb. Place the lamb in a Pyrex baking dish large enough for both lamb and marinade. Pierce the lamb all over with a large tined fork. Turn the lamb over and pierce again.

Roughly chop the onion and lemon and place in a food processor. Add the remaining ingredients to processor. Process until finely chopped but not to a purée.

Pour the marinade over the lamb and rub into top surfaces. Turn the lamb over and rub into the other side. If the marinade does not cover the lamb, add more wine and pomegranate juice. Cover with plastic wrap and refrigerate for 1 to 3 days. Turn the lamb about 4 times a day.

When ready to cook, remove from the refrigerator and allow to warm a little.

Prepare the charcoal for grilling, or heat a gas grill. Remove the lamb from marinade and scrape off any excess. Reserve the marinade.

Grill the lamb on medium heat until 145° in the thickest part for medium-rare. The thinner sections will be more done.

Meanwhile, strain the marinade and place in a saucepan. Add 1 cup of Pinot Noir and simmer rapidly to reduce to about 1½ cups. If sauce is too thin, thicken with a Tbsp. of cornstarch thinned with a Tbsp. of Pinot Noir.

Let the lamb rest for about 10 minutes, then carve and serve with the wine sauce.

COOKING SECRETS: A 5 to 6 lb. whole leg of lamb will yield about 3 to 4 lbs. when boned, butterflied and trimmed. Pomegranate juice can be found at Middle Eastern specialty grocery shops.

Jack Duey
Cooper Mountain Vineyards
Beaverton, Oregon

Lamb Kebobs

Prepare the marinade in a large mixing bowl by combining the oils, lemon juice, vinegar, garlic, salt, pepper and maple syrup. Marinate the lamb for 4 to 6 hours for best results.

Skewer 4 oz. portions of the lamb onto 9-inch bamboo skewers. Flatten the kebobs so they need cooking on 2 sides only. Charbroil on medium-high heat to a medium doneness, approximately 130° to 140° internal temperature.

COOKING SECRETS: Good vegetable dishes to complement are Sesame Snow Peas, Charbroiled Asparagus or eggplant or Mediterranean Green Beans. Garnish the plates with a good quality chutney.

Kathleen Kodak
Ashland Vineyards and Winery
Ashland, Oregon

Serves 4
Preparation Time:
45 Minutes (note marinating time)

Bone 1 leg of lamb into ¾-inch cubes. Save trim for another use.
¾ cup peanut oil
¼ cup extra-virgin olive oil
4 Tbsps. lemon juice
4 Tbsps. white wine vinegar
2 Tbsps. garlic purée
Salt and pepper to taste
2 Tbsps. maple syrup

Marinated Rack of Lamb with Minted Jus

Serves 4 to 6
Preparation Time:
20 Minutes (note marinating time)
Pre-heat oven to 400°

- **4 to 6 large lamb racks (7–8 bones)**
- **1 medium onion, roughly chopped**
- **6 large cloves garlic**
- **1 tsp. cracked black pepper**
- **2 cups olive oil**

Place the onion, garlic and pepper in a food processor and purée. Add the olive oil and blend until smooth, about 1 minute.

Place small amount of this marinade in the bottom of a 9″×13″ container. Alternate cleaned and frenched racks (save lamb trim) with marinade. Marinate for a minimum of 12 hours, up to 72 hours.

Arrange racks well spaced on a baking sheet. Bake at 400° for 40 minutes, for medium-rare. Size of racks may vary cooking time, so check for doneness along the bone line half way through cooking and every 5 minutes after.

Remove meat from oven and let rest for at least 10 minutes.

Serve lamb drizzled with the minted jus.

COOKING SECRET: The lamb is delicious with garlic roasted baby potatoes and fresh asparagus as accompaniments. I recommend a Petite Sirah or a fruity Merlot.

Minted Jus

Minted Jus
Preparation Time:
3 Hours

- **Trim from lamb racks**
- **1 carrot**
- **2 stalks celery**
- **½ onion**
- **3 cups water**
- **1 Tbsp. cornstarch**
- **2 Tbsps. mint sauce**
- **Salt and pepper**

Roast the lamb trim in a 300° oven until dark brown with the carrot, celery, onion, and water, simmering for 3 hours. Strain and reduce the sauce by half. Thicken slightly with cornstarch and season with mint sauce. Adjust seasonings with salt and pepper.

Dory Ford
April Point Lodge
Campbell River, British Columbia

Pacific Rim Lamb

Serves 6
Preparation Time:
1½ Hours (Note Marinating Time)
Cooking Time: 1 Hour

- **2 cups Pinot Noir**
- **½ cup olive oil**
- **⅓ cup soy sauce**
- **1 Tbsp. garlic, minced**
- **2 Tbsps. fresh ginger, grated**
- **1 tsp. cumin**
- **1 tsp. cracked black pepper**
- **6 lbs. leg of lamb, boned and butterflied**

Combine the Pinot Noir, oil, soy, garlic, ginger, cumin and pepper in a glass or non-aluminum pan. Add the lamb. Marinate 6 to 12 hours, covered and refrigerated. Turn occasionally to coat.

Broil in oven or grill on barbecue 5 to 6 inches from heat source until lamb reaches desired doneness, 40 to 45 minutes for medium rare. Baste with marinade throughout cooking. Let meat rest for 15 minutes before carving.

COOKING SECRET: Serve with small red potatoes, oven roasted and tossed with melted butter and chopped rosemary.

Marj Vuylsteke
Oak Knoll Winery, Inc.
Hillsboro, Oregon

Saddle of Lamb with Tarragon Mustard Sauce

Serves 4
Preparation Time:
45 Minutes

2 Tbsps. Dijon mustard
½ oz. fresh tarragon
¼ cup veal stock or demi-glace
2 Tbsps. olive oil
8 lamb chops
2 Tbsps. unsalted butter
¼ cup brandy
Salt and pepper to taste

In a mixing bowl, combine the mustard and tarragon with the veal stock. Set aside.

Heat olive oil in saucepan over medium-high heat. Add lamb. Sauté lamb chops in single layer, turning when uniformly brown, about 4 minutes on each side for medium rare.

Pull the lamb from the pan, add the butter and flame with brandy. Add the veal stock and reduce by half.

To serve, spoon the sauce onto plate. Slice the lamb and fan over sauce.

COOKING SECRET: Serve with garlic-roasted red potatoes and sautéed mustard greens.

Donald Alcorn and Andrew Elarth
Al Boccalino Ristorante
Seattle, Washington

Spit-Roasted Herb-Rubbed Leg of Lamb with Mint & Walnut Pesto Glaze

The day before serving, place the lamb in a large container and rub all over with the herb rub. Refrigerate for 24 hours.

Roast the leg bone at 350° for 20 minutes. Place in a large pan with chopped vegetables and water, simmer for 2 hours. Strain, pouring the lamb stock into a large fry pan. Reduce by three-fourths or more, depending on the desired flavor. Reserve.

Place the lamb on a spit and cook at medium-high heat for approximately 45 minutes.

While the lamb is cooking, place the mint, oil and walnuts in a food processor. Blend until somewhat smooth.

Place the lamb stock and mint pesto in a small pot. Bring to a boil. Simmer until the sauce coats the back of a spoon. Remove the lamb from the spit. Let stand for 20 to 30 minutes.

Serve the lamb with the mint walnut pesto.

Herb Quinn
Raintree Restaurant
Gastown, Vancouver, British Columbia

Serves 8
Preparation Time:
30 Minutes (Note Marinating Time)
Cooking Time: 4 Hours

1 medium-sized fresh leg of lamb, boned, with leg bone reserved
¼ cup herb rub (recipe follows)
1 carrot, chopped
1 onion, chopped
2 stalks celery, chopped
1 tomato, chopped
4 cups water
1 lb. fresh mint or 1 small jar of mint sauce
¼ cup olive oil
¼ cup walnuts, toasted

Herb Rub

- 1 Tbsp. dried thyme
- 1 Tbsp. dried oregano
- 1 Tbsp. dried sage
- 1 Tbsp. dried rosemary
- ¼ Tbsp. fennel seed
- ½ Tbsp. coriander
- 1 bay leaf
- ¼ Tbsp. lavender
- Zest of 1 lemon
- Zest of 1 orange
- 1 Tbsp. balsamic vinegar
- 4 Tbsps. Kosher salt
- ¼ cup olive oil
- 1 Tbsp. black pepper

oast all the dried herbs in a hot skillet. Pulse briefly in a coffee grinder or food mill, then combine with the fruit zest, vinegar, salt, oil and pepper.

Herb Quinn
Raintree Restaurant
Gastown, Vancouver, British Columbia

Stuffed Lamb Chops

With a small sharp knife make a ½-inch incision into the lamb chops directly behind the bone.

In a large mixing bowl, combine the minced lamb, pine nuts, parsley, currants, cumin, mint, egg, garlic and salt and pepper to taste. Holding the chop firmly in one hand, stretch the opening in the lamb chops with the index finger of your other hand to form a larger cavity and stuff approximately 4 Tbsps. of the mixture into each chop. Pinch the opening shut to keep the stuffing inside.

Grill the chops over low to medium heat for approximately 5 minutes on each side, or, sear off in a heavy skillet to brown both sides and finish in a 325° oven for 15 minutes until medium well.

To make the sauce, combine the vinegar, sugar, wine and raspberries in a saucepan and bring to a boil Simmer to reduce by ¼. Strain through a fine mesh sieve and serve with the stuffed lamb chops.

Serves: 6
Preparation Time:
45 Minutes

12 lamb chops, trimmed
1¼ lb. lean minced lamb
½ cup pine nuts, toasted
½ cup parsley, chopped
¼ cup dry currants
¼ tsp. cumin
1 Tbsp. fresh mint, chopped
1 egg, lightly beaten
2 garlic cloves, minced
Salt and pepper to taste
¼ cup aged balsamic vinegar
1 Tbsp. sugar
¼ cup red wine
½ cup raspberries
2 cups brown veal stock

Denis A. Blais
Monterey Lounge & Grill
Pacific Palisades Hotel
Vancouver, British Columbia

☆

Pork Tenderloin with Cabernet Port Sauce

Serves 4
Preparation Time:
30 Minutes (Note Marinating Time)
Cooking Time: 1 Hour

- **2 lb. pork tenderloin**
- **Yoshida's Gourmet Sauce for marinade**
- **Salt and pepper to taste**
- **1 cup Tefft Cellars Cabernet Sauvignon**
- **½ cup Tefft Cellars Port**
- **½ cup Yoshida's Gourmet Sauce**
- **2 Tbsps. butter**

Marinate the pork tenderloin in Yoshida's Gourmet Sauce at least 2 hours before cooking, preferably overnight. While your barbecue is warming up, open a bottle of Tefft Cellars Cabernet Sauvignon and enjoy a glass. Salt and pepper the meat and grill it for approximately 40 minutes or until done to your liking.

To prepare the sauce, bring 1 cup of Tefft Cellars Cabernet Sauvignon to a boil and reduce it by half. Then add ½ cup each of Tefft Cellars Port and Yoshida's Gourmet Sauce and turn down the heat to a simmer. When the sauce has reduced by half, turn off the heat and stir in 2 Tbsps. of butter to thicken the sauce.

Allow the tenderloin to cool for 10 minutes before liberally applying the sauce. Now it is time to sit down with friends and enjoy the meal and the rest of the wine.

Pam and Joel Tefft
Tefft Cellars
Outlook, Washington

Pork Tenderloin Stuffed with Wild Mushrooms

Dice the trimmings from the pork tenderloin and pound in a mortar to a coarse paste.

Melt the butter in a saucepan, adding the shallots and cooking over low heat for 5 to 8 minutes or until thoroughly soft. Add the pancetta and mushrooms and cook another 10 minutes or until all the water the mushrooms have released is reabsorbed. Add the garlic and cook 1 minute.

Turn the mixture onto a cutting board and coarsely chop. Combine the mushroom mixture with the herbs. Season with salt and a liberal grinding of pepper.

Make a slit down each pork tenderloin. Stuff with half of the mushroom mixture.

Preheat a 12" skillet on low heat. Place the tenderloins in the pan with the olive oil and brown on all sides slowly. Remove the tenderloins to a 400° oven and roast until done, about 5 to 10 minutes. Let rest 5 minutes.

To make sauce, deglaze the pan with the chicken stock, allowing liquid to reduce to about ¼ cup. Swirl in the butter.

To serve, slice the tenderloin on the bias and garnish with sauce.

COOKING SECRET: This is delicious over mashed potatoes.

Catherine Whims
Genoa
Portland, Oregon

Serves 4
Preparation Time:
45 Minutes
Pre-heat oven to 400°

2 pork tenderloins, trimmed
Salt and pepper
2 Tbsps. butter
¼ cup shallots, finely diced
2 oz. pancetta, diced
½ lb. fresh porcini or other wild mushrooms
1 large clove garlic
2 Tbsps. fresh Italian parsley, chopped
½ tsp. fresh thyme, chopped
2 Tbsps. olive oil
Salt and pepper to taste
1 cup chicken stock
2 Tbsps. butter

Grilled Stuffed Pork Chop

Serves 6
Preparation Time:
1 Hour

- **8 1½ inch thick center cut pork chops**
- **8 slices fontina cheese, 1 oz. each**
- **16 fresh sage leaves**
- **1 red onion, finely chopped**
- **2 Tbsps. olive oil**
- **½ cup black currants**
- **½ cup toasted pine nuts**
- **¼ cup balsamic vinegar**
- **1 cup reduced veal or chicken stock**
- **¼ lb. unsalted butter**
- **1 tsp. fresh thyme**
- **Salt and pepper to taste**

Cut pockets into the pork chops and stuff each with a slice of fontina cheese wrapped around 2 sage leaves. Grill over charcoal fire for 30 minutes.

To prepare the sauce, sauté the onion in a large sauté pan with olive oil for 5 minutes. Add the currants, pine nuts and vinegar and reduce briefly. Add the stock and reduce by half. Add the butter and seasonings.

To serve, pour the sauce over the pork chops.

David Machado
Pazzo Ristorante
Portland, Oregon

Roasted Loin of Pork with, Pears and Vino Santo

Sauté the shallots in a medium-size saucepan until lightly browned. Add the pears and sweat. Deglaze with Vino Santo and reduce down to a syrup-like consistency. Add the demi glace and simmer. Skim as needed. Strain through a ultra-fine chinois-type strainer. Slowly add butter just before serving.

Season the pork loin with cracked peppercorns. Roast whole in a 400° oven until the pork loin reaches an internal temperature of 150°. Allow to rest for 10 to 15 minutes.

Serve the pork drizzled with the sauce.

Serves 4
Preparation Time:
45 Minutes
Pre-heat oven to 400°

3 each shallots, peeled and chopped
2 each pears, diced
1 bottle Vino Santo or red wine
4 cups demi glace of pork or veal
2 tsps. Butter
2½–3 lb. boneless pork loin
Peppercorns, ground, optional

Walter Pisano
Tulio
Seattle, Washington

Roasted Pork Tenderloin with a Rhubarb, Mustard Purée

Serves 4
Preparation Time:
One Hour
Pre-heat oven to 350°

- **1½ lbs. rhubarb, diced**
- **½ cup port wine**
- **¼ cup honey**
- **1 Tbsps. Dijon mustard**
- **½ cup pureéd and strained marionberries, fresh or frozen**
- **3 pork tenderloins, approximately 12 oz. each**
- **1 Tbsp. olive oil**
- **Salt and pepper to taste**

In a stainless or ceramic saucepan, bring the rhubarb, wine, honey and mustard to a simmer until the rhubarb is thoroughly tender, about 15 to 20 minutes. Stir several times to avoid scorching. Remove from heat.

Add the berry purée to taste, adding more honey and mustard if necessary.

Rub the meat with olive oil, a little mustard, salt and pepper. Brown the meat on all sides in a frying pan on medium heat. Place on a rack in roasting pan and place in a 350° oven for about 20 minutes or until a meat thermometer inserted into the thickest part of the meat registers 170°. Remove from oven, cover loosely with foil and let rest for 5 minutes.

Meanwhile gently reheat the sauce and reduce slightly to thicken. Adjust the seasoning.

To serve, arrange sliced pork on top of the sauce.

Mark Manley
Union Bay Café
Seattle, Washington

☆

Great Gravy Pot Roast

Serves 6
Preparation Time:
1 Hour
Cooking Time: 2–2½ Hours

- 3 to 4 lb. chuck or boneless sirloin roast
- Salt and pepper to taste
- 1 clove garlic, finely chopped
- 1 large carrot, cut in strips
- 1 large onion, sliced
- ¾ cup Hoodsport Merlot
- ¾ cup dairy sour cream, at room temperature
- ½ cup water
- 2 to 3 Tbsps. flour
- 1 Tbsp. lemon juice

Rub the meat with salt and pepper and brown on all sides over high heat. Add the garlic, carrot, and onion. Cook until the onion is golden brown, about 3 minutes.

Reduce the heat and stir in the wine and sour cream. Cover tightly and cook over low heat (liquid barely simmering) for 2 to 2½ hours or until the meat is tender.

Remove from heat. Skim off fat from the pan juices. Mix water and flour into a smooth paste. Add to the pan juices, stirring until thickened. Add a little boiling water if the gravy is too thick. Stir in the lemon juice.

COOKING SECRET: Serve with mashed potatoes, tossed salad and Hoodsport Merlot or Island Belle wine.

Peggy and Edwin Paterson
Hoodsport Winery
Hoodsport, Washington

Roast Prime Rib with Cabernet Sauce

Serves 6
Preparation Time: 45 Minutes
Cooking Time: 4½ Hours
Pre-heat oven to 325°

- **½ cup peanut or olive oil**
- **1 cup yellow onion, chopped**
- **1 cup carrots, chopped**
- **⅓ cup parsley, chopped**
- **1 bay leaf**
- **1 tsp. thyme**
- **½ cup flour**
- **2 cups Cabernet Sauvignon**
- **2 qts. beef stock or canned broth**
- **2 Tbsps. tomato paste**
- **¼ tsp. fresh ground black pepper**
- **¼ cup dry sherry**
- **Salt to taste**
- **4 to 6 lb. boneless or tied rib roast**

Heat ¼ cup oil over medium heat in a heavy 3 to 4 qt. stockpot. Add the onions, carrots, and parsley, stirring until they begin to brown. Add the bay leaf and thyme and reduce to a low simmer.

In a sauté pan, add ¼ cup oil and the flour and stir until light brown. Stir this roux into the simmering vegetables and add the remaining ingredients to the stockpot except the sherry, salt and meat. Bring to a boil, then reduce the heat to a heavy simmer and cook uncovered about 2 hours or until it has reduced by half.

Add the sherry and salt to taste and simmer for 5 minutes. Strain before serving.

Season the meat and roast in a shallow pan at 325° for approximately 2½ hours or until desired doneness. Remove from oven and allow to rest for at least 1 hour before carving. Serve the prime rib sliced, topped with a small serving of the Cabernet sauce.

Pam and Joel Tefft
Tefft Cellars
Outlook, Washington

☆

Baked Ribs in Barbecue Sauce

In a saucepan, lightly brown the onions in oil. Add all the remaining ingredients and simmer for 15 minutes. While the sauce is simmering, prepare ribs.

Place ribs in a roasting pan. Pour the prepared barbecue sauce over ribs and bake at 350° for 30 to 45 minutes or until tender.

Adolf Kruger
Wild Goose Vineyards and Winery
Okanagan Falls, British Columbia

Serves 4
Preparation Time:
45 Minutes
Pre-heat oven to 350°

- **4 lbs. loin back ribs**
- **1 cup onions, chopped**
- **¼ cup oil**
- **1 cup tomato sauce**
- **½ cup water**
- **2 Tbsps. prepared mustard**
- **¼ cup brown sugar**
- **¼ cup lemon juice**
- **3 Tbsps. Worcestershire sauce**
- **2 tsps. salt**
- **¼ tsp. pepper**
- **½ cup fresh parsley**

Crockpot Cabernet Roast

Serves 4
Preparation Time:
6 Hours

- **1¼ cups Cabernet Sauvignon or other dry red wine**
- **½ cup stone-ground type prepared mustard.**
- **6 carrots, peeled, quartered lengthwise, cut in half**
- **2 large onions, cut into lengthwise sections**
- **1 boneless chuck or other pot roast, about 3 lbs.**

Mix the Cabernet and mustard together in a crockpot. Add the carrots, onions and pot roast. Cook about 6 hours on high or longer on low, turning the roast once during cooking.

Remove the roast to a serving platter, surround with carrots and onions and keep warm.

Pour the meat juices into a pan and reduce until slightly thickened. Use as sauce to serve over roast.

Ann Williams
Kiona Vineyards and Winery
Benton City, Washington

Veal and Prawn Involtini

Cut veal into 4 equal pieces, taking care to slice across the grain of the meat. Using two pieces of plastic wrap with the veal in the middle, pound the veal with a meat mallet until almost transparent. Lay pieces of veal side by side, and sprinkle with salt and pepper. Place two pieces of basil on top of each slice of veal and top with a tiger prawn.

Starting at one end, roll the veal around the tiger prawn. Place the rolled veal and tiger prawns side by side and skewer through the center of each.

Place fry pan on medium high heat and add the vegetable oil. Dust the skewered veal and tiger prawns with flour and when the oil is hot enough, place in the pan and cook for 2 minutes on each side, to sear the veal. Discard any excess oil and grease from fry pan.

Add the shallots, garlic, lemon, red wine and veal stock to the pan with the veal rolls and place in a 425° oven to finish cooking for 10 to 15 minutes.

Remove the veal rolls from the pan and return to the pan to top of stove at medium to high heat. Reduce the sauce until it is of a thick consistency, adding a teaspoon of butter just before the sauce is done.

To serve, slice each veal and prawn roll into three equal pieces and fan them, 2 per plate, finishing with the sauce drizzled over the top.

Serves 2
Preparation Time:
45 Minutes
Pre-heat oven to 425°

8 oz. veal tenderloin
Salt and pepper to taste
8 fresh basil leaves
4 large tiger prawns
1 Tbsp. vegetable oil
½ cup flour
1 whole shallot, chopped
2 garlic cloves, chopped
Juice of ½ lemon
¼ cup dry red wine
½ cup of veal stock
1 tsp. butter

Gino Punzo
Café de Medici Restaurant
Vancouver, British Columbia

Natural Veal Medallions

Serves 2
Preparation Time:
30 Minutes

- **6 veal medallions, 2 oz. each, lightly pounded**
- **1 cup flour**
- **½ cup olive oil**
- **¾ cup mushrooms (shiitake, oyster or portobella)**
- **1 garlic clove, chopped**
- **1 shallot, chopped**
- **1 Tbsp. Dijon mustard**
- **2 Tbsps. gherkins, chopped**
- **¼ cup brandy**
- **½ cup demi-glace**
- **Salt and white pepper**

Lightly pound the veal medallions and dredge them in flour. Set aside.

Heat ¼ cup of the olive oil in sauté pan, add the mushrooms, garlic and shallots and sauté for 2 to 3 minutes. Add the Dijon and gherkins and sauté 2 to 3 minutes.

Add the brandy and demi-glace and simmer 5 to 10 minutes.

As the sauce simmers, heat the remaining olive oil in large sauté pan until hot and add the lightly floured veal to the pan. Salt and pepper.

Cook 2 minutes over medium heat, turn and cook 2 to 3 minutes more. Remove from pan to a serving platter and top with the mushroom sauce.

Andrew Mueller
Chez Jeannette
Gleneden Beach, Oregon

Main
Courses

Steamed Buns with a Savory Seafood Filling Served with a Carrot Juice Glaze and Scallion Oil Infusion Sauce

Serves 4
Preparation Time:
3 Hours

- **3 cups all-purpose flour**
- **¼ cup fresh tarragon, chopped**
- **1½ tsps. yeast**
- **2 Tbsps. white sugar**
- **½ cup unrefined corn oil**
- **1 cup warm water**
- **Unrefined corn oil, organic if possible**
- **6 fresh tarragon tops**
- **1 tsp. baking powder**
- **½ cup all-purpose flour**
- **1 sheet, 9×12″ silicon baking paper**
- **Seafood filling, recipe follows**

Place the flour, tarragon, yeast and sugar in a large mixing bowl. Make a well in the center and pour in 1 Tbsp. of the oil and warm water. Use a large wooden spoon and mix until a ball of dough is formed.

Place the dough on a floured work surface and knead for 8 minutes or until the dough is soft and elastic.

Transfer the dough to an oiled bowl and brush with corn oil. Cover with a cloth or plastic wrap and allow to triple in bulk (approximately 1½ hours) in a warm place.

Punch down the dough. Form into a 3-inch diameter roll and cut into six equal portions. Cover the work surface with baking powder and extra flour and shape each portion into a flat disk about six inches in diameter. Stretch the edges to make them thinner.

Place ⅓ cup of the filling into the center and fold the edges to completely enclose the filling and pinch tightly to seal. This will form a round ball.

Place the sealed bottom (not the side you have pinched closed) down on a sheet of 4″×6″ silicon baking paper. Brush each bun with corn oil and decorate with one tarragon sprig. Allow this to rise double in volume.

Place the buns into a Chinese bamboo steamer or stainless steel vegetable steamer on high heat, for 10 minutes.

To serve, cut the steamed bun into 4 pieces and arrange them in the center of the plate to show off the filling. Drizzle the carrot glaze (recipe follows) around the bun. Drizzle 1 Tbsps. of the green onion oil throughout the glaze in a random pattern.

Frederique & Sinclair Philip
Sooke Harbour House
Sooke, British Columbia

Seafood Filling

Place the salmon chunks in a food processor and process until smooth. While the processor is still running, gradually add the egg white, garlic, shallots and cream in a slow stream. Transfer this mousse into a medium-sized mixing bowl. Place this bowl inside a larger bowl filled with ice.

Combine the white wine and fennel seeds in a small saucepan, bringing this mixture to a simmer over medium heat. Remove from the heat, and allow to steep for later use.

Gently incorporate the chopped shrimp, chopped herbs and strained fennel seed mixture with the use of a rubber spatula until a smooth homogeneous mixture is achieved. Chill until ready to fill buns.

To make the carrot juice glaze, reduce 3 cups of the carrot juice to 2 cups over high heat. Add the vinegar. Dissolve the cornstarch in the remaining ¼ cup carrot juice. Beat the cornstarch-carrot juice mixture into the simmering liquid and cook for 5 minutes over medium heat. Whisk frequently. Add the ¼ cup chopped herbs.

To make the scallion oil, place the oil in a blender bowl. With the motor running on high, feed the green ends of the onions into the blender and allow to blend for 2 to 3 minutes. Strain the onion oil through a fine sieve into a 2-cup jar.

Add 2 tbs. of the separated onion pulp to the strained oil in the jar. Refrigerate for up to two weeks and store in a dark place or opaque container.

¾ lb. fresh salmon filet, deboned, cut into 1-inch chunks
1 egg white, chilled
1 garlic clove, peeled, finely chopped
1 shallot, finely diced
¾ cup whipping cream
¼ cup Sémillon wine
1 Tbsp. fresh fennel seeds
6 fresh large shrimps, shells and heads removed, chopped
1 Tbsp. fresh tarragon sprigs, finely chopped
1½ Tbsps. Italian parsley, finely chopped
½ Tbsp. fresh lemon thyme, chopped
1 tsp. salt
3¼ cups of carrot juice
2 Tbsps. apple cider vinegar
2 tsps. cornstarch
¼ cup chopped herbs, cilantro, parsley, chives
2 cups sunflower seed oil
2 bunches green onions

Frederique & Sinclair Philip
Sooke Harbour House
Sooke, British Columbia

☆

Pork Stir Fry

Serves 4
Preparation Time:
30 Minutes

- **1 Tbsp. cornstarch**
- **3 Tbsps. water**
- **1 Tbsp. soy sauce**
- **1 tsp. ginger root, finely grated**
- **1 tsp. salt**
- **4 Tbsps. oil (not olive oil)**
- **½ to ¾ lbs. lean pork chops, cut into 3-inch long strips less than ¼ inch in diameter**
- **¼ tsp. liquid smoke**
- **Dash of hot pepper sauce**
- **Splash of Riesling wine**
- **1 lb. sliced vegetables (bok choy, bean sprouts, water chestnuts, onions, snow peas, and mushrooms)**

Make the sauce by mixing the cornstarch with water. Add the soy sauce, ginger root, and salt.

Heat two 2 Tbsps. of oil in a wok to fragrance. If it smokes, turn down the heat. Carefully add the pork and stir to keep it from sticking.

Add the liquid smoke and hot pepper sauce. Fry until well done. Remove and keep warm.

De-glaze the wok with a splash of Riesling wine.

Add 2 more Tbsps. of oil to the wok and heat. Add the vegetables in order, mushrooms last because they overcook quickly.

When the vegetables are done, add the pork. Add the sauce and mix well while heating to a boil.

Place in a heated serving dish and serve at once.

COOKING SECRET: Keep the size of the vegetables consistent so that the pieces cook simultaneously. Things that require more cooking time are added first and those that require the least are added last, so that everything is still crisp but cooked when the whole dish comes together at the end.

Gail & Shirley Puryear
Bonair Winery
Zillah, Washington

☆

Warm Oregon Bleu Cheese Tart

In a food processor, mix the flour, salt, and sugar. Cut in the butter to the mixture. Add the eggs and milk and process until a ball forms. Wrap and chill for 30 minutes or overnight.

When dough has thoroughly chilled, roll it out on a floured surface until very thin. Line a 12-inch springform pan with dough and line dough with aluminum foil. Add pie weights or loose dried beans and bake at 350° until golden, about 30 minutes. Let cool.

To make the filling, pass the cheese through a sieve into a bowl to make very fine crumbles. Add the cream and egg yolks and mix well. Season with salt and pepper, add thyme to taste. Let mixture sit at room temperature for about an hour.

Correct the seasoning. Pour the mixture into the shell and bake at 350° until set like jelly, about 25 minutes. Let rest 10 minutes before serving.

COOKING SECRET: Serve the tart with baby greens and toasted hazelnuts or walnuts dressed with extra virgin olive oil or hazelnut oil.

Serves 8
Preparation Time:
1½ Hours (note refrigeration time)

1½ cups flour
1 tsp. salt
2 Tbsps. sugar
2 sticks (1 cup) + 1 Tbsp. unsalted butter
2 eggs
2 Tbsps. milk
4½ cups crumbled bleu cheese
2 cups heavy cream
6 egg yolks
Salt and pepper to taste
Freshly chopped thyme to taste

Klaus Monberg
Jarboe's
Manzanita, Oregon

☆

Pasta
&
Grains

Duck with Cabernet Cherry Sauce over Angel Hair Pasta

Pierce the skin side of each breast with a fork then season with salt and pepper.

Add the olive oil to a hot heavy skillet, then brown the breasts skin side down (to render excess fat) for 3 minutes. Turn, brown the other side for 1 minute, then remove the duck to drain. Reduce heat to medium-high, drain off all but 1 Tbsp. of duck fat, then sauté the onion and garlic until soft.

Add the veal stock, Cabernet Sauvignon, celery, rosemary, parsley, nutmeg, cherries, sugar and tomato paste. Bring to a boil, add salt and pepper to taste, and simmer until the sauce is reduced by a third.

Add the duck breasts to the sauce and simmer, covered, for 20 minutes. Remove breasts and slice ⅜ inch thick. Pour sauce over angel hair pasta, top with sliced duck and garnish with chopped radicchio.

Serves 4
Preparation Time:
45 Minutes

- **4 duck breasts, boned with skin on**
- **Salt and freshly ground black pepper to taste**
- **2 Tbsps. olive oil**
- **1 large onion, thinly sliced**
- **2 garlic cloves, chopped**
- **1 cup veal stock**
- **1 cup Cabernet Sauvignon**
- **1 Tbsp. celery leaves, chopped**
- **1 tsp. fresh rosemary, chopped**
- **1 Tbsp. Italian parsley, chopped**
- **⅛ tsp. nutmeg, grated**
- **½ cup Chukar cherries, dried and pitted**
- **Pinch of sugar**
- **1½ Tbsps. tomato paste**
- **½ lb. angel hair pasta, cooked, drained**
- **Radicchio, finely chopped, garnish**

John Sarich
Chateau Ste. Michelle
Woodinville, Washington

☆

Westport Crab and Shrimp Cannelloni with Hazelnut Pesto

Serves 4
Preparation Time:
45 Minutes
Preheat oven to 325°

- **2 Tbsps. extra virgin olive oil**
- **1 cup red pepper strips, roasted**
- **1 lb. Dungeness crab meat**
- **1 lb. shrimp, cooked, chopped**
- **1 Tbsp. fresh Italian parsley, chopped**
- **1 clove garlic, chopped**
- **¼ cup grated Romano cheese**
- **Splash of Chardonnay wine**
- **¼ tsp. freshly ground black pepper**
- **Salt to taste**
- **4 cannelloni pasta, 2½ to 3-inches wide sheets**
- **1 cup tomato or marinara sauce**

Hazelnut Pesto

- **3 cups tightly packed fresh basil leaves**
- **1 cup tightly packed fresh Italian parsley leaves**
- **4 garlic cloves**
- **1 cup extra virgin olive oil**
- **¼ cup Parmesan cheese, grated**
- **2 Tbsps. hazelnuts, roasted, chopped**
- **Salt to taste**

In a blender or food processor, purée the olive oil with the roasted red peppers. Add the crab, shrimp, parsley, garlic, Romano cheese, Chardonnay, black pepper and salt. Pulse until gently combined.

In 2 qts. boiling water, cook the pasta until al dente, then rinse under cold running water and lay flat. Thinly spread the seafood mixture over the pasta and roll up. Place in a buttered baking dish.

Add the tomato or marinara sauce around the pasta, then bake for 10 to 12 minutes, or until heated through.

To serve, slice the cannelloni into 1½-inches widths. Spread Hazelnut Pesto on plates and top with sliced cannelloni.

Hazelnut Pesto

To a blender or food processor, add the basil, parsley, garlic and olive oil a little at a time, blending until the mixture has a loose paste consistency. Add the cheese and hazelnuts. Salt to taste, then blend until smooth.

John Sarich
Chateau Ste. Michelle
Woodinville, Washington

Crème Fettuccine

Melt the butter and sauté the garlic until soft. Stir in the flour and cook for 1 to 2 minutes. Slowly add the Chardonnay, stirring constantly, then add the cream, tomatoes, and dill. Simmer 5 to 10 minutes. Salt and pepper to taste.

Stir the steamed vegetables into the hot fettuccine, then add the sauce and seafood. Toss until mixed well.

Serve on warm plates, topped with Parmesan cheese and toasted hazelnuts.

COOKING SECRET: This dish is delicious with Oak Knoll Chardonnay or Riesling.

Serves 6
Preparation Time:
30 Minutes

- **6 Tbsps. butter**
- **2 cloves garlic, minced**
- **1 tsp. flour**
- **1 cup Chardonnay**
- **1 cup cream**
- **¾ cup tomatoes, seeded, chopped**
- **½ cup fresh dill, minced**
- **Salt and pepper to taste**
- **3 cups steamed vegetables (asparagus, mushrooms and red pepper)**
- **1 lb. fettuccine, cooked al dente**
- **¾ cup cooked shrimp or crab**
- **Freshly grated Parmesan cheese**
- **Toasted hazelnuts**

Marj Vuylsteke
Oak Knoll Winery, Inc.
Hillsboro, Oregon

Fettuccine with Caramelized Onions, Prosciutto and Herbs

Serves 4
Preparation Time:
15 Minutes

- **4 Tbsps. olive oil**
- **2 medium onions, thinly sliced lengthwise**
- **1 lb. fresh fettuccine**
- **2 Tbsps. soft. butter**
- **1 bunch Italian parsley leaves, roughly chopped**
- **1 Tbsp. fresh sage leaves, finely chopped**
- **1 Tbsp. fresh oregano, finely chopped**
- **1 tsp. rosemary, finely chopped**
- **½ cup Parmesan cheese, grated**
- **4 oz. thinly sliced prosciutto, julienne**
- **Fresh ground black pepper**

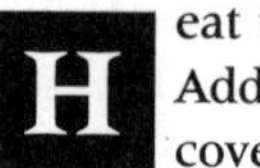
Heat the olive oil in large sauté pan on medium heat. Add the onions and stir. Turn down the heat and cover. Cook slowly, stirring occasionally, until onions are soft and fragrant.

Remove the lid and turn up the heat to brown the onions, stirring to avoid burning, as the flavor will be bitter. When the onions are a light caramel color, remove from heat and set aside.

In boiling salted water, cook, then drain, the fettuccine. Toss with the onions, butter and herbs.

Divide into warm bowls, and top each with Parmesan cheese, prosciutto and a grind of fresh black pepper.

Tom Martino
Il Bistro
Seattle, Washington

Linguine with Dungeness Crab

Sauté the garlic, tomatoes, basil and chile flakes in 2 Tbsps. olive oil over medium heat, about 1 minute or until the tomatoes become thick.

Add the crab meat.

Add the cooked pasta and toss with 2 Tbsps. olive oil.

Serves 4
Preparation Time: 15 Minutes

- **4 garlic cloves, crushed**
- **½ cup fresh plum tomatoes, chopped**
- **2 Tbsps. fresh basil, cut in strips**
- **Pinch of crushed red chile flakes**
- **4 Tbsps. extra-virgin olive oil**
- **¾ lb. Dungeness crab meat**
- **1 lb. linguine, cooked al dente**
- **Salt and pepper to taste**

Donald Alcorn and Andrew Elarth
Al Boccalino Ristorante
Seattle, Washington

☆

Penne & Sausage with Vodka Sauce

Serves 4
Preparation Time:
2½ Hours
Pre-heat oven to 450°

- **6 mild Italian link sausages**
- **2 Tbsps. unsalted butter**
- **1 medium onion, chopped**
- **1½ tsps. red pepper flakes**
- **2 cans plum tomatoes, 12 oz. each, with liquid**
- **1 cup vodka**
- **1½ tsps. tomato paste**
- **1 lb. penne pasta**
- **1 cup Parmesan cheese, coarsely grated**
- **Fresh ground pepper to taste**
- **Fresh oregano or parsley, chopped, for garnish**

In a large pot, bring water to boil. Add the sausage links to boiling water. Turn off heat and let stand.

In a heavy-bottomed saucepan, melt the butter. Add the onion and red pepper flakes. Cook over medium-low heat until the onion is translucent.

Stir in the whole tomatoes with liquid and simmer for 1 hour. Add the drained sausage links and vodka and continue to cook at a simmer for another hour. Turn heat to high, add cream and tomato paste and stir constantly for 10 minutes. Reduce to a simmer and cook for 30 minutes.

Meanwhile, bring 4 quarts of water to boil in a large pot. Drop the pasta in the boiling water and cook, stirring frequently, until al dente.

Drain well and toss the pasta and sauce in a casserole with ⅔ cup Parmesan cheese. Bake for 10 minutes at 450°. Remove from oven and sprinkle with remaining cheese. Sprinkle with fresh chopped oregano or parsley and serve.

COOKING SECRET: The sauce can be made a day in advance and freezes well. Use as a main dish with a simple green salad, crusty bread and Tuscan wine. Serve over angel hair pasta, with or without sliced sausage, for a pasta course.

David Marth
3 Doors Down
Portland, Oregon

Butternut Squash Ravioli with Hazelnut-Sage Butter Sauce

Roast squash at 400° for 40 minutes; discard seeds and skin.

Sauté the onion in 1 Tbsp. olive oil until golden. When the onions have cooled, combine the onions with the squash, ricotta cheese, egg, and seasonings in a food processor. Process for one minute.

Stuff the sheets of egg pasta with the squash mixture to make the ravioli. Seal pasta edges and plunge in boiling salted water for 1 to 2 minutes or until the raviolis are cooked al dente.

For the sauce, sauté the hazelnuts in 1 Tbsp. olive oil with the shallots for two minutes. Add the Marsala and reduce. Add the butter. While stirring, add the sage and salt and pepper to taste.

Serve ravioli on a pool of sauce. Sprinkle with Parmesan before serving.

David Machado
Pazzo Ristorante
Portland, Oregon

Serves 4
Preparation Time:
45 Minutes
Pre-heat oven to 400°

- 1 butternut squash
- 1 small onion, finely chopped
- 2 Tbsps. olive oil
- 1 cup ricotta cheese
- 1 egg
- Salt, pepper and nutmeg to taste
- 1 lb. fresh sheets of egg pasta
- ½ cup toasted, ground hazelnuts
- 1 Tbsp. shallots, chopped
- ¼ cup Marsala wine
- ½ cup unsalted butter
- 1 Tbsp. fresh sage, chopped
- Salt and pepper to taste
- Freshly grated Parmesan cheese

Goat Cheese Ravioli with Bay and Sage

Serves 4
Preparation Time:
45 Minutes (note refrigeration time)

- **2 cups all-purpose unbleached flour**
- **3 eggs, beaten**
- **8 oz. mild goat cheese, cubed**
- **¼ lb. Gruyere cheese, cubed**
- **2 Tbsps. heavy cream**
- **1 egg, beaten**
- **2 Tbsps. fresh chervil, rosemary or chives, finely chopped**
- **Salt and freshly ground pepper to taste**
- **1 cup chicken stock**
- **1 cup heavy cream**
- **6 bay leaves, preferably fresh**
- **Salt and freshly ground black pepper**
- **Large handful of fresh sage, rinsed and patted dry**

Prepare the pasta by placing the flour in a food processor with a steel blade. With the machine running, add 2 beaten eggs slowly until the eggs and flour form pea-sized shapes but before dough forms a ball. You may not need all of the egg mixture. Turn out and knead for 1 minute. It should feel stiff, not sticky. Wrap in plastic wrap and let rest 1 hour before rolling on the pasta machine.

In the bowl of a food processor fitted with a metal blade, combine the goat cheese, Gruyere cheese, cream, and 1 beaten egg, and process until well blended. Add the herbs, salt and pepper, and blend again. Adjust seasonings to taste.

Prepare the ravioli by taking one section of dough and, using a pasta machine, roll the dough very thick. Fold the dough in half. On one half of the dough place teaspoonfuls of filling about an inch apart. Spray dough or brush with water. Fold other half of dough over and press between filling to seal. Cut ravioli with a ravioli cutter and make certain they are sealed.

In a large, shallow skillet that will hold all the pasta later on, combine the stock, cream and bay and sage leaves. Bring to a boil over high heat. Reduce by half.

Meanwhile, bring a large pot of water to a boil. Salt the water and add the ravioli and cook until just tender. Drain.

Add the ravioli to the cream mixture and toss to coat with the cream. Sprinkle generously with pepper and serve immediately.

Catherine Whims
Genoa
Portland, Oregon

Seafood Risotto

Heat 2 tsps. olive oil in a large pot over medium-high heat. Cook the shallots and garlic in oil, stirring frequently, until the shallots are crisp-tender. Reduce heat to medium. Stir in rice. Cook, stirring frequently until rice begins to brown. Stir in the wine. Cook until the liquid is absorbed.

Pour ½ cup of the broth over the rice mixture. Cook uncovered, stirring occasionally, until liquid is absorbed.

Continue cooking 15 to 20 minutes, adding broth ½ cup at a time and stirring occasionally, until rice is tender and creamy.

When the rice mixture is just about ready, heat 2 tsps. of oil in a small skillet over medium heat. Cook the scallops and shrimp in oil 3 to 4 minutes, stirring frequently, until the shrimp are pink. Remove the scallops and shrimp from the skillet and gently stir the seafood into the cooked rice mixture along with the lemon peel.

Sprinkle risotto with parsley before serving.

COOKING SECRET: This elegant yet easy dish is perfect with French bread, crisp tossed salad and a chilled glass of Chasselas wine.

Gina Adams
Quails' Gate Estate Winery
Kelowna, British Columbia

Serves 4
Preparation Time:
30 Minutes

4 tsps. olive oil
¼ cup shallots, finely chopped
2 garlic cloves, finely chopped
1 cup arborio rice
½ cup white wine
2½ cups vegetable or chicken broth
¼ pound raw scallops, medium-sized
¼ pound raw shrimp, medium-sized, peeled and deveined
1 tsp. grated lemon peel
2 Tbsps. fresh parsley

☆

Vegetables
&
Side Dishes

Roasted Beets with Fresh Cherry Sauce

Place beets in a heavy pan. Cover with foil and roast in the oven until a knife goes through them easily. Depending on the size of beets, this could take 15 to 40 minutes. When cool enough to handle, slip the skins off and remove the tops (leave a little on top if beets are very small). Cut into rounds or wedges, or leave whole, depending on size. Beets can be roasted the day before serving, if you like.

Wash and pit the cherries. Set aside.

Sauté the onion in olive oil until transparent.

Place cherries in a food processor with onion, parsley, basil, dill and vinegar and purée. Pour into a fine strainer over a small saucepan and drain well. When as much liquid is removed from pulp as possible, set this aside in a small bowl. Over medium-high heat, reduce the liquid down to ¼ cup or less. Pour into the pulp, mix well, season the sauce to taste with salt and pepper.

Spoon the cherry sauce over the beets before serving.

Serves 4
Preparation Time:
40 Minutes
Pre-heat oven to 350°

2 lbs. fresh beets of uniform sizes, any variety
1½ cups fresh cherries (Bing, Rainier, or any variety that's tree-ripe and sweet)
¼ onion, finely chopped
1 Tbsp. Italian parsley, finely chopped
1 Tbsp. Thai basil, chiffonade
2 tsps. dill, chopped
Salt and black pepper to taste
2 tsps. wine vinegar

Laura Dewell
Pirosmani
Seattle, Washington

☆

Port Wine Braised Mushrooms

Serves 6
Preparation Time:
30 minutes

- **1 lb. small white mushrooms, cleaned**
- **1 cube butter (½ cup)**
- **½ cup lightly packed brown sugar**
- **¾ tsp. black pepper**
- **1½ tsps. thyme**
- **1 to 1½ cups port wine**
- **½ cup sour cream**

Sauté the mushrooms in butter over medium heat. Sprinkle with brown sugar and simmer until the sugar is dissolved. Add the seasonings.

Cover with port wine and simmer 10 to 15 minutes. Add the sour cream and simmer 10 minutes.

Dawn Kindred
The Manor Farm Inn
Poulsbo, Washington

Sorrel and Spinach Pie

Butter 4 large muffin tins and set aside.

In a heavy-bottomed sauce pot, bring chicken stock to a simmer with onion, nutmeg, 2 Tbsps. of the clarified butter, salt and pepper. Reduce liquid to 1 cup and remove from heat. Add eggs and stir well. Return to heat and cook, stirring occasionally, until eggs are scrambled and quite dry.

Meanwhile, squeeze the spinach and then sorrel until most of the moisture is gone. When egg mixture is ready, add crumbled feta and pine nuts, stirring until cheese melts. Season again with salt and pepper. Distribute this mixture equally between the spinach and sorrel and mix well. Season again if necessary.

Cut phyllo into 5″×5″ squares. Cover with plastic wrap and, working with two at a time, place two pieces of phyllo a few inches apart on work surface and brush with clarified butter. Place another sheet directly over this and again brush with butter. Then with 6 more layers, with butter between each layer, lay them out to look like a pinwheel. Place these over the muffin tins and gently press one and then the other down inside the tins. Cover with plastic wrap while you do the other two.

Distribute sorrel mixture evenly between the phyllo cups. Then do the same with the spinach mixture, pressing down gently each time to remove any air pockets. Enclose any phyllo that is overhanging. Brush tops with butter, and cover with foil.

Bake 10 minutes at 400°, then remove foil and finish baking until tops are well browned, about 5 minutes. Remove from oven and turn out of molds onto a dry cookie sheet or cooling rack. Cool 5 minutes before serving.

Laura Dewell
Pirosmani
Seattle, Washington

Serves 4
Preparation Time: 45 Minutes
Pre-heat oven to 400°

- **2 cups chicken stock**
- **1 medium onion, thinly sliced**
- **2 pinches nutmeg**
- **1 cup clarified butter, very warm**
- **Salt and freshly ground black pepper to taste**
- **5 eggs, beaten**
- **2½ lbs. fresh spinach, steamed and drained**
- **2½ lbs. fresh sorrel, steamed and drained**
- **¾ cup feta cheese, crumbled**
- **¼ cup pine nuts, lightly toasted**
- **1 box phyllo dough**

Stilton Spiked Polenta

Serves 4
Preparation Time:
40 Minutes (Note Standing Time)

- **2 Tbsp. olive oil**
- **1 tsp. garlic, minced**
- **1 tsp. shallot, minced**
- **1 tsp. fresh ground black pepper**
- **1 Tbsp. fresh herb mixture (thyme, oregano, savory, etc.)**
- **2½ cups vegetable/chicken stock**
- **1 cup cornmeal**
- **¼ lb. Stilton cheese**

Heat oil in a medium saucepan over medium heat. Add the garlic, shallots, pepper and herbs and sauté until the garlic is slightly browned. Add the stock and bring to a boil. When the stock is boiling, add the cornmeal by pouring in slowly, using a whisk at first to avoid lumping, then continue to stir with spoon or spatula.

The cornmeal mixture will get thick, so turn down the heat and stir until the texture is smooth, about 2 minutes.

Crumble the stilton into the polenta, stir and remove from heat.

Pour into a buttered baking sheet. Let sit for at least 1 hour.

Cut into portions and bake to rewarm at 350° for 20 minutes.

Harry McWatters and Bob Wareham
Sumac Ridge Estate Winery
Summerland, British Columbia

Cilantro Marinated Prawns with Cauliflower Tahini & Curried Lentils

Combine the mint, 1 cup cilantro and olive oil in a blender and purée until smooth. Pour into a container and add the prawns. Let marinate for 24 hours in the refrigerator. Remove from the marinade and drain. In a sauté pan with a slight coating of oil, cook the prawns over medium-high heat until flesh turns pink, approximately 2 minutes. Remove from heat.

For the cauliflower tahini, bring 2 qts. of salted water to a boil in a saucepan. Add the cauliflower and cook until fork-tender. Drain well and plunge in a bowl of iced water. Drain well. In a blender, purée 1 Tbsp. garlic, tahini paste, cumin, lemon juice and water until smooth and paste-like. More water may needed. Season with salt and pepper. This is best to make one day in advance.

In a saucepan, heat the olive oil over medium heat. Add the onion, 1 Tbsp. garlic, ginger and jalapeño, and cook until onions become translucent, 3 to 5 minutes. Add the spices and incorporate well. Add the lentils and stock, and bring to a boil. Lower heat and simmer for 6 to 8 minutes. Remove the lentils from heat and swirl in butter. If there is too much liquid, drain the lentils prior to adding the butter. Stir in 3 Tbsps. chopped cilantro. Spoon curried lentils onto each serving plate, top with a dollop of cauliflower tahini and 4 shrimp.

Monique Barbeau
Fullers
Seattle, Washington

Serves 4
Preparation Time:
1½ Hours (Note Marinating Time)

1 cup mint leaves
1 cup + 3 Tbsps. cilantro
1 cup olive oil
16 prawns, peeled, deveined
¼ head cauliflower, cut into flowerettes
2 Tbsps. garlic, chopped
2 oz. tahini paste
1½ tsp. cumin
Juice of 1½ lemons
1 tsp. water
Salt and pepper to taste
2 Tbsps olive oil
½ onion, diced
1 Tbsps. ginger, grated
1 small jalapeño, minced
1 tsp. ground cinnamon
2 bay leaves
2 Tbsps. curry powder
1 cup French green lentils, cooked
3 cups chicken stock
2 Tbsps. butter, cold and cubed

☆

Coconut Blancmange with Apricot Coulis

Brûlée Au Chocolat

Chocolate Truffle Cake

Hazelnut Meringue Cake with Chocolate Cinnamon Cream

Lemon Pudding Cake

Fresh Oregon Berry Compote with Orange Sabayon

Summer Berry Compote

Gelato al Caffe

Chocolate Cabernet Kisses

Mango Mousse

Pastry Star Filled with Anise Ice Cream & Topped with Chocolate Sauce

Poached Pear with Rhubarb Sauce

Riesling Poached Pears with Vanilla Custard Sauce

Sunburnt Lemon Pie

Cinnamon Hazelnut Bread Pudding

Chocolate Roulade with Fresh Strawberries

Boysenberry and Peach Shortcakes with Honey Whipped Cream

Old-Fashioned Gingersnaps

Frozen Mocha Soufflé with Cinnamon Syrup

Blackberry Strudel with Frangelico Custard Sauce

Almond Peach Tart

Chocolate Hazelnut Tart

Mixed Nut Tart

Cabernet Truffles

☆

Coconut Blancmange with Apricot Coulis

In a mixing bowl, combine the cornstarch, ½ cup sugar and salt in a bowl over boiling water. Add the milk and 1½ cups coconut milk to this mixture. Stir until thick and smooth. Add 1½ cups shredded coconut and cover.

Cook for 15 minutes. Add the vanilla and almond extracts and remove from heat and cool. Do not refrigerate.

When cool, beat in mixing bowl and fold in the whipped cream. Chill.

Make macadamia nut crumbs by placing macadamia nuts in the food processor and process until finely chopped. Add the remaining ¾ cup shredded coconut, just to blend. Set aside.

In a saucepan combine the apricots, ¼ cup sugar and Amaretto over low heat. Simmer for 10 minutes.

When blancmange is cool, layer into wine glasses alternating with the coconut crumbs. Start and end with crumbs. Serve with the apricot coulis.

Serves 6
Preparation Time:
45 Minutes

4 Tbsps. cornstarch
¾ cup sugar
⅛ tsp. salt
2 cups milk
1½ cup coconut milk
2¼ cups shredded coconut
1 tsp. vanilla
1 tsp. almond extract
¾ cup heavy cream, whipped
¾ cup macadamia nuts
1 lb. apricots, peeled, seeded, sliced
¼ cup Amaretto

Sean Seedlock
Chez Shea
Seattle, Washington

Brûlée Au Chocolat

Serves 6
Preparation Time:
2½ hours (Note Refrigeration Time)
Pre-heat oven to 350°

- **8 oz. bittersweet chocolate**
- **8 egg yolks**
- **4 whole eggs**
- **¾ cup granulated sugar**
- **½ tsp. salt**
- **1 tsp. vanilla extract**
- **1 qt. heavy cream**
- **6 to 8 Tbsps. light brown sugar**

or the brûlée custard, chop the chocolate into small pieces. Melt over a double boiler and keep warm until needed.

In a mixing bowl, whisk together the egg yolks, whole eggs, sugar, salt and vanilla extract, until the sugar is dissolved and all ingredients are thoroughly blended.

In a medium-size saucepan, scald the cream, then whisk in the melted chocolate until thoroughly combined. Whisk the chocolate and cream into the egg/sugar mixture.

Through a fine mesh sieve, strain the custard to remove any bits of egg that may have coagulated during mixing. Use at once, or cool to room temperature and refrigerate for up to a week before use.

To bake the custard, pour the prepared custard into one-cup ramekins, filling each three-quarters full. Place the ramekins in a deep, waterproof baking dish. Pour water into the baking dish, filling it to two-thirds of the way up the sides of the ramekins.

Place baking dish in a 350° oven and bake until the custards test clean (a knife inserted off-center comes out clean), approximately 55 to 60 minutes. Do not overbake; the custards will set up as they cool.

Remove the baking dish from the oven and lift the ramekins from the water bath. Set aside to cool to room temperature before refrigerating at least 3 hours, preferably overnight. Do not refrigerate the custards while warm, or cover them even when cool, as this may cause condensation to form on the surface of the custard.

At least 1 hour before serving, pre-heat oven to 350°. Spread the brown sugar on a cookie sheet and place it in the oven. Turning the oven off, keep the sugar inside approximately 20 minutes, then remove from the oven and cool. This process will dry the sugar, making it easier to sift. Sift the dried sugar evenly onto the tops of the custards. Place the custards under a hot broiler until the sugar caramelizes and starts to bubble. Remove and allow to cool a minute or two before serving.

John Zenger
River Place Hotel
Portland, Oregon

Chocolate Truffle Cake

Melt the chocolate on low power in a microwave. Add the melted butter.

In a mixing bowl, beat the egg yolks with the vanilla until light in color, about 5 minutes. Mix in the coffee and cognac. Add the chocolate to the egg yolks and set aside.

Whip the egg whites with cream of tartar until foamy. Add the sugar and beat until glossy. Using a wire whisk, fold a big scoop of egg whites into the chocolate mixture. Then fold in the rest of the egg whites.

Bake in an oiled 9-inch springform pan for 1 hour at 350°. Cool.

COOKING SECRET: Serve with fresh berries, berry coulis, caramel, or vanilla sauce.

Serves 10 to 12
Preparation Time: 1¼ Hours
Pre-heat oven to 350°

- **8 oz. chocolate**
- **¾ cup sweet butter, melted**
- **6 egg yolks**
- **1 tsp. vanilla**
- **¼ cup strong coffee**
- **2 Tbsps. cognac and/or orange liquor**
- **8 egg whites**
- **¼ tsp. cream of tartar**
- **¾ cup sugar**

Cecilia Hughes
Willcox House
Bremerton, Washington

Hazelnut Meringue Cake with Chocolate Cinnamon Cream

Serves 8
Preparation Time:
1½ Hours
Pre-heat oven to 350°

- **1⅓ cups hazelnuts**
- **5 large egg whites**
- **1¼ cups powdered sugar**
- **2½ cups whipping cream**
- **14 oz. bittersweet chocolate, chopped**
- **½ tsp. ground cinnamon**

Butter a 9-inch springform pan with 2¾-inch sides. Coarsely grind the hazelnuts in a food processor. Whip the egg whites to soft peaks in a large mixing bowl. Gradually add the sugar. Beat until stiff. Fold in the nuts and pour into a springform pan. Smooth the top. Bake at 350° until the top is firm and center not too soft, about 1 hour. Cool on a rack.

In a saucepan bring ¾ cup whipping cream to a boil and turn it off. Add the chocolate and stir until melted and homogenous. Add the cinnamon. Cool to room temperature.

Whip the remaining cream until stiff. Fold into the chocolate mixture.

To assemble, cut the meringue free from the sides of the pan with a paring knife and remove the ring. Using a serrated knife, split the meringue into half horizontally. Place 1 layer cut-side down on a plate. Spread the filling over the bottom layer. Place the second layer on top. Do not refrigerate. Store at room temperature until ready to serve.

COOKING SECRET: This dessert is exceptionally good served with a fresh raspberry sauce.

Klaus Monberg
Jarboe's
Manzanita, Oregon

Lemon Pudding Cake

Serves 4
Preparation Time:
One Hour
Pre-heat oven to 350°

- **3 eggs, separated**
- **1 cup sugar**
- **4 Tbsps. butter, melted**
- **⅓ cup flour**
- **⅓ cup lemon juice**
- **Zest of 1 lemon, grated**
- **1 cup milk, warm**

Beat the egg yolks with ½ cup sugar and melted butter in a large mixing bowl. Add the flour and lemon juice. Mix in the grated lemon zest.

In a separate bowl, beat the egg whites until foamy. Add ½ cup sugar and beat until glossy.

Add the warm milk to the egg yolk mixture. Fold the whites and the yolk mixture together.

Bake in a 2 to 3 qt. ovenproof bowl, set in a pan of hot water, at 350° for 45 minutes or until the top is lightly browned.

Serve with fresh berries. Raspberries are an excellent choice.

Cecilia Hughes
Willcox House
Bremerton, Washington

Fresh Oregon Berry Compote with Orange Sabayon

Serves 4
Preparation Time:
20 Minutes (Note Refrigeration Time)

2 oranges
7 large egg yolks
2 Tbs. Marsala
1 cup heavy cream

Zest oranges and mince the zest. Squeeze the juice from oranges.

Place the orange zest, orange juice, egg yolks and Marsala, in a double boiler over medium heat. Whisk the sabayon mixture until the eggs are pale yellow. Do not overcook.

Remove from heat and place in a ice bath to cool. Then fold in the cream and refrigerate.

1 cup marionberries
1 cup raspberries
1 cup blueberries
1 cup strawberries
1 Tbsp. balsamic vinegar

Rinse berries under cold running water. Core the strawberries and quarter. Place all the berries and vinegar in a stainless mixing bowl and let marinate for 1 hour.

To serve, divide berries into 4 small bowls and spoon the sabayon over the top.

Greg Meixner
Bay House
Lincoln City, Oregon

Summer Berry Compote with Hazelnut Ice Cream

Combine the wine, sugar and pepper in a saucepan over high heat and bring to a boil Add the berries and reduce heat to low. Simmer only until berries are heated through.

Divide the berries into 6 bowls. Place two scoops of ice cream over each mound of berries. Garnish with lemon balm and serve immediately.

Serves 6
Preparation Time: 10 Minutes

- **½ cup Riesling wine**
- **2 Tbsps. sugar**
- **One grind black pepper**
- **3 cups fresh berries, such as strawberries, blackberries, raspberries, etc.**
- **Vanilla or Hazelnut Ice Cream**
- **6 leaves lemon balm**

Howard Soon
Calona Vineyards
Kelowna, British Columbia

Gelato al Caffe

Serves 4
Preparation Time:
40 Minutes (Note Refrigeration Time)

- **3 cups whipping cream**
- **1 cup whole coffee beans**
- **½ cup very concentrated espresso**
- **9 egg yolks, beaten**
- **¾ cup superfine sugar**

In a double boiler mix 2 cups cream, the coffee beans, and the concentrated espresso and cook over rapidly boiling water for at least 30 minutes, or until the cream shows small bubble around the edges and tastes strongly of coffee.

Whisk the yolks gradually in to the hot cream and coffee beans, whisking rapidly to prevent the yolks from curdling. Set the bowl of yolks and cream over the boiling water and cook, whisking constantly, until the mixture has thickened.

Remove from the heat and add the sugar. Set the bowl into a slightly larger bowl of crushed ice and place in the refrigerator for at least 2 hours. The custard should be very well chilled before it's put in the freezer.

When ready to freeze the ice cream, strain out the coffee beans and add 1 cup cream. Freeze.

Catherine Whims
Genoa
Portland, Oregon

☆

Chocolate Cabernet Kisses

Melt the chocolate and butter in the top of a double boiler over gently simmering water, stirring until smooth. Stir in ⅓ cup Cabernet. Set aside to cool.

Combine the sugar, water and corn syrup in a heavy saucepan, mixing well. Stir until the mixture boils. Cover and cook 3 minutes until the steam has washed down any crystals which may have formed on the sides of the pan. Cook, uncovered over medium heat, without stirring, until the mixture reaches the soft ball stage at 234°. Remove from the heat.

Beat the egg whites until very stiff. Gradually add the hot syrup to the whites, continuing to beat at least 5 minutes, until the mixture thickens and cools.

Gently but thoroughly, fold the chocolate and egg white mixtures together. Lightly butter a large sheet of parchment paper. Using a 6B or other pastry tip, pipe the "kisses" onto the parchment. Cool.

Yields 40 Kisses
Preparation Time:
30 Minutes

1 lb. bittersweet or semi-sweet chocolate
4 Tbsps. unsalted butter
⅓ cup Cabernet Sauvignon
6 Tbsps. sugar
1 Tbsp. water
⅓ cup light corn syrup
2 egg whites

Pat Lee
Henry Estate Winery
Umpqua, Oregon

☆

Mango Mousse

Serves 6
Preparation Time:
15 Minutes (Note Refrigeration Time)

- **2 pkgs. unflavored gelatin**
- **2 cups fresh mango purée (about 2 large mangoes)**
- **½ tsp. vanilla**
- **⅓ cup sugar**
- **2 cups plain yogurt**

Sprinkle the gelatin over ½ cup cold water in a saucepan, allowing the gelatin to bloom. Dissolve slowly over low heat or in a microwave.

Purée the mango, vanilla and sugar in a blender or food processor. Fold in the yogurt and dissolved gelatin.

Pour into individual custard cups. Chill before serving.

COOKING SECRET: A easy desert to prepare the day before.

Peggy Kuan
Chanticleer Inn
Ashland, Oregon

Pastry Star with Anise Ice Cream Topped with Milk Chocolate Sauce

To make the pastry star, bring to a simmer over low heat ½ cup water, 4 Tbsps. butter, a pinch of salt and a pinch of sugar. Add the flour and beat with a wooden spoon until the mixture is smooth and comes away from the side of the pan.

Slowly add 2 eggs until the mixture has a creamy, thick consistency. This can be done easier with the help of a mixer.

Place in a piping bag with a small, plain nozzle. Pipe the mixture onto a baking sheet, covered with silicone paper, into the shape of a star.

Bake at 425° for 6 minutes, then 350° for 6 minutes, 325° for 6 minutes, and 300° for 6 minutes. Turn off the oven and keep the door ajar for 20 minutes for the pastry to dry.

Prepare the ice cream by infusing the star anise and vanilla bean in ½ pt. cream. DO NOT BOIL. Whisk ¼ cup sugar and 6 egg yolks into the mixture until the color is a pale yellow, then add the hot milk. Whisk every 10 minutes until mixture is cool.

Once cool, strain and place in an ice cream machine until semi frozen, about 15 minutes. Place in freezer for 12 hours.

Prepare the chocolate sauce by melting the chocolate in a double bain-marie until melted. In a separate saucepan combine 2 Tbsps. cream, 1 cup milk, 2 Tbsps. sugar and 2 Tbsps. butter and bring to a boil. Remove from heat and stir in the chocolate until smooth. Strain and cool.

Prepare the caramel garnish by boiling 1 cup sugar and ½ cup water until the temperature is 291°. Cool for a few minutes and then pour onto the silicone sheets into desired shapes. (At the restaurant we do this in the shape of a star.) Once the caramel has set, about 10 minutes, place in an airtight container until set.

To serve, cut the pastry in half and fill with the anise ice cream, top with the milk chocolate sauce and garnish with the caramel star.

Julian Bond
Star Anise Restaurant
Vancouver, British Columbia

Serves 4
Preparation Time:
2 Hours (Note Refrigeration Time)
Pre-heat oven to 425°

1 cup water
6 Tbsps. butter
Pinch of salt
Pinch of sugar
⅓ cup flour
2 eggs
6 whole star anise
1 vanilla bean
½ pt. + 2 Tbsps. cream
1½ cups sugar
6 egg yolks, room temperature
7 oz. milk chocolate
2 Tbsps. cream
1 cup milk

Poached Pear with Rhubarb Sauce

Serves 4
Preparation Time:
45 Minutes
Pre-heat oven to 350°

- **4 medium-sized ripe pears**
- **4 oz. light cream cheese, room temperature**
- **1 Tbsp. honey**
- **¼ tsp. vanilla**
- **2 Tbsps. vanilla-flavored yogurt, optional**
- **5 medium stalks of rhubarb, cut into ½-inch pieces**
- **1–2 cups water**
- **1 cup sugar**
- **Raspberries, optional**
- **Powdered sugar, garnish**
- **1 tsp. nutmeg**

Cut pears in half and remove the seeds and stem. Place the pears cut side down in a 9×13 inch baking pan which has ½-inch water in it. Bake at 350° degrees for 20 to 30 minutes.

Remove the pears from dish and place on glass serving dish, cut side up. Let cool.

In a mixing bowl, combine the cream cheese, honey, and vanilla until smooth. Add the yogurt if a smoother texture is desired.

Place cut pieces of rhubarb in medium-sized saucepan with 1 to 2 cups water, depending upon the size of the rhubarb stalks. The water should cover about half the rhubarb when it's in the pan. Bring to a boil, stir in sugar, cover the saucepan, and turn off the heat. Let the pan stay on the burner until cool. Add raspberries if desired for a brighter color. After the sauce cools, stir thoroughly, and add more sugar and nutmeg to taste.

To serve, place 1 Tbsp. of the cream cheese mixture in the center of each pear. Drizzle the rhubarb sauce over the top. Garnish with sprinkled powdered sugar and fresh nutmeg.

Carol McGough
The James House
Port Townsend, WA

Riesling Poached Pears with Vanilla Custard Sauce

Combine the water, sugar and Riesling in a large pot. Bring to a boil and boil for 5 minutes. Reduce the heat to medium-low and add the pears. Simmer until the pears are tender but not mushy, about 5 to 10 minutes. Remove from heat and let pears cool in the syrup. Set aside.

Prepare the vanilla custard sauce in a large saucepan over high heat, by combining the milk and vanilla bean. Bring the mixture to a boil, then remove from heat. Cover and set aside to infuse, about 15 minutes.

Using an electric mixer, whisk the egg yolks and sugar in a separate bowl until thick and lemon-colored, approximately 3 to 4 minutes. Set aside.

Return the milk mixture to a high heat; bring to a hot simmer, but do not allow to boil. Pour a little of the simmering milk into the egg mixture, whisking constantly as milk is added. Return the milk-egg mixture to milk in the saucepan. Place over low heat and cook, stirring constantly with a wooden spoon until mixture thickens, about 2 minutes. Do not boil. Sauce should be the consistency of thick cream.

Discard the vanilla bean and strain the sauce through a fine mesh sieve into a clean bowl. Place the bowl into a larger ice-filled bowl or tub to stop the cooking. Stir occasionally to speed up the cooling process. Once cooled, cover securely and refrigerate.

To serve, portion the custard sauce among four plates. Cut the pears in half lengthwise, then slice from bottom to top, not cutting all the way through the stem. Fan pear halves onto the pools of custard sauce and garnish with mint leaves. Serve slightly chilled.

COOKING SECRET: This dish is delicious with a Riesling wine.

Mike Caldwell
Flerchinger Vineyards
Hood River Valley, Oregon

Serves 4
Preparation Time:
45 Minutes (Note Refrigeration Time)

2 cups water
½ cup sugar
2 cups Riesling
4 ripe pears, peeled
2 cups milk
1 plump, moist vanilla bean, split lengthwise
6 egg yolks
½ cup granulated sugar
Mint leaves (optional)

Sunburnt Lemon Pie

Serves 8
Preparation Time:
45 Minutes (Note Refrigeration Time)
Pre-heat oven to 350°

1 cup all-purpose flour
1 cup sugar
⅓ cup butter
7 eggs
1 Tbsp. orange juice
1 tsp. orange rind, grated
¾ cup whipping cream
½ cup fresh lemon juice
2 tsps. vanilla extract
1 tsp. lemon peel, grated

In a food processor, combine the flour and ¼ cup sugar. Using an on/off motion, cut in the butter until the mixture resembles coarse meal.

In a small bowl, combine 1 egg, orange juice and orange rind. Add to the flour mixture. Mix just until dough forms a ball. Refrigerate dough for 20 minutes.

Press dough into greased 11-inch flan pan. Place pan on a baking sheet. Cover the pie with parchment paper and fill with pie weights. Bake pie shell for 20 minutes or until the center is set. Remove the weights and paper.

To prepare the lemon filling, set aside 1 Tbsp. sugar from the ¾ cup sugar. In a bowl, whisk together 6 eggs and remaining sugar. Whisk in whipping cream, lemon juice, vanilla and lemon peel until smooth.

Pour into shell. Bake for 30 minutes. Let cool. Sprinkle reserved 1 Tbsp. sugar over pie. Cover the pie edges with foil and broil for about 3 minutes or until the sugar is brown and caramelized.

COOKING SECRET: Serve plain or with your favorite coulis. Orange and raspberry are my choices.

Pierre Delacote
Seasons in the Park Restaurant
Portland, Oregon

☆

Cinnamon Hazelnut Bread Pudding

Place the raisins into a one cup measuring cup. Add the Frangelico, and fill to one-cup level with warm water. Let soak for 10 to 15 minutes.

Brush toasted bread with melted butter on both sides. Cut slices into quarters. Place quarters into buttered 9×13 inch baking dish.

Blend the sugar, nutmeg, and hazelnuts in a small mixing bowl. Spread the applesauce over the bread pieces, then sprinkle the sugar-spice mixture over the top.

Drain the raisins, reserving the liquid, and evenly drop over the sugar and spice layer.

In a separate bowl, blend the half & half, eggs, reserved raisin liquid, and vanilla. Pour over the other ingredients in a baking dish.

Bake in a preheated oven at 350° for 35 to 40 minutes.

Serve warm, with fresh whipped cream or half & half. Also a great breakfast treat or afternoon snack.

Serves 6
Preparation Time:
One Hour
Pre-heat oven to 350°

½ cup raisins
¼ cup Frangelico (hazelnut liqueur)
8 slices white bread, toasted
½ cup butter, melted
½ cup brown sugar
2 tsps. nutmeg
½ cup finely ground hazelnuts
1½ cups applesauce
3 cups half & half
5 eggs
1½ tsps. vanilla
Whipped cream, optional

Kevin Spanier
The Lion and The Rose
Portland, Oregon

☆

Chocolate Roulade with Fresh Strawberries

Serves 8
Preparation Time: 45 Minutes
Pre-heat oven to 425°

- **¼ cup water**
- **⅓ cup cocoa powder**
- **1 tsp. vanilla**
- **3 large egg yolks**
- **⅔ cup sugar**
- **½ cup cake flour**
- **½ tsp. salt**
- **4 large egg whites**
- **½ tsp. cream of tartar**
- **1 pt. whipping cream**
- **Powdered sugar**
- **2 pts. strawberries**
- **¼ cup Late Harvest Riesling**
- **Fresh mint leaves, garnish**

Line a jelly roll pan with parchment paper, grease the paper and dust lightly with flour.

Bring the water to a boil in a small saucepan. Remove the pan from the heat and add the cocoa and vanilla and stir until smooth. Set aside to cool.

In a large bowl, beat the egg yolks and ⅓ cup sugar with an electric mixer until the mixture is pale and slightly thick. Add the cocoa mixture and beat until thick again. Add the flour and salt and beat again, about 1 minute.

In a separate bowl with clean beaters, beat the egg whites until foamy. Add the cream of tartar and continue beating until the whites begin to hold a soft peaks. Add the remaining sugar and beat until the whites hold a stiff and glossy peak.

Stir ¼ of the egg whites into the cocoa mixture to loosen the mixture, then fold in the remaining egg whites, being careful not to deflate them too much.

Spread the batter gently into the prepared jelly roll pan. Bake the cake at 425° for about 8 minutes or until it springs back when lightly touched. Let the cake cool in the pan, then cover the cake with a damp kitchen towel. Invert the cool cake onto the kitchen towel and gently peel off the parchment paper. Starting with a narrow end, roll the cake up in jelly roll fashion with the towel inside and set aside until ready to fill.

Whip the whipping cream until stiff. If a sweeter filling is desired, add ¼ cup powdered sugar and blend into cream. Slice the strawberries and toss lightly with the Late Harvest Riesling, reserving a few whole berries for decoration.

To fill the roulade, unroll the cake but leave it on the dish towel. Spread the whipped cream evenly over the cake. Starting at the small end, roll the cake in a jelly roll fashion. Transfer the roulade to a platter, cover and chill well until ready to serve.

To serve, dust the whole cake with powdered sugar. Slice the roulade and top with sliced strawberries. Garnish with whole strawberries and fresh mint leaves.

John and Sherita Weisinger
Weisinger's of Ashland Vineyard and Winery
Ashland, Oregon

Boysenberry and Peach Shortcakes with Honey Whipped Cream

Sift together the flour, salt, 3 Tbsps. sugar and baking powder in a large mixing bowl for the shortcakes. Add the butter and citrus zest, mixing until the mix ture resembles coarse cornmeal with occasional pea-sized chunks of butter.

Add 1¼ cups cream and work gently until the dough just holds together. Pat the dough to a 1-inch thickness and cut to the desired shape. Brush with cream and sprinkle with sugar. Bake at 375° for 12 to 15 minutes until golden brown.

Score the skin of the peaches with a sharp knife and drop them in boiling water for 5 to 10 seconds. Remove with a slotted spoon and drop in ice water. Peel the peaches and slice them 1-inch thick. Combine with ¼ cup sugar and heat in heavy sauce-pan until the fruit just comes to a boil. Cool and reserve for the dessert.

Whip the remaining 2 cups cream with the honey until very fluffy.

To serve, split the shortcakes with a sharp knife. Spoon on a generous dollop of honey whipped cream. Spoon on the cooled peaches and sprinkle generously with fresh ripe boysenberries. Drizzle with Creme de Cassis and top with the other half of the shortcake. Serve with an excellent Blanc de Noir Champagne.

Eric Lenard
Hunt Club-Sorrento Hotel
Seattle, Washington

Serves 4
Preparation Time:
Pre-heat oven to 375°

3 cups flour
¾ tsp. salt
¼ cup + 3 Tbsps. sugar
2 Tbsp. baking powder
6 oz. sweet butter, cold and cut in small cubes
Zest of one lemon and one orange
3¼ cups cream
4 cups ripe peaches
¼ cup sugar
2 Tbsps. honey
2 cups boysenberries
2 Tbsp. Creme de Cassis

☆

Old-Fashioned Gingersnaps

Yields: 4 dozen
Preparation Time: 30 Minutes
Pre-heat oven to 300°

1½ cups shortening
2 cups sugar
½ cup molasses
2 eggs
4 cups flour
4 tsps. baking soda
2 tsps. ginger
2 tsps. cloves
2 tsps. cinnamon
Granulated sugar

In a large bowl, mix together the shortening, sugar, molasses and eggs.

In another bowl, sift together the flour, baking soda, ginger, cloves and cinnamon.

Add the flour mixture to the wet ingredients. Mix well.

Shape into large walnut-sized balls, then roll in granulated sugar. Bake at 300° for 15 minutes on lightly greased cookie sheet.

Richard and Judy Shinton
Hudson House Bed and Breakfast
Cloverdale, Oregon

Frozen Mocha Soufflé with Cinnamon Syrup

To make the syrup, combine the coffee, sugar and cinnamon stick in a saucepan over medium-high heat. Reduce the mixture until it reaches a syruplike consistency.

Heat the milk with ⅔ cup sugar and ground coffee. Stir to dissolve the sugar. Add the chopped chocolate, stirring constantly over very low heat until the chocolate is completely melted.

In a separate bowl, mix the egg yolks with ⅓ cup sugar. Temper the yolks with the chocolate mixture. Return to the saucepan and cook over low heat for 5 minutes. Strain into a metal bowl which is resting in a bowl of ice. Cool the mixture.

Whip the cream and fold into the chocolate mixture when it is cold. Pour into individual soufflé dishes and place in a freezer for at least 8 hours. This step may be done several days ahead. Before serving, place in refrigerator for 1 to 2 hours to allow to soften.

To serve, unmold the soufflé and drizzle with the cinnamon syrup.

Serves 6
Preparation Time:
35 Minutes (Note Refrigeration Time)

6 cups coffee
1 cup sugar
1 stick of cinnamon
2 cups homogenized milk
⅔ cup sugar
⅓ cup ground coffee
3 oz. semi-sweet chocolate, chopped
6 egg yolks, beaten
⅓ cup sugar
1 cup whipping cream

Marilyn & Johnathan Chilvers
Oceanwood Country Inn
Mayne Island, British Columbia

Blackberry Strudel with Frangelico Custard Sauce

Serves 4
Preparation Time:
30 Minutes (Note Refrigeration Time)
Pre-heat oven to 350°

- **4 cups blackberries, fresh if possible**
- **1½ cups sugar**
- **½ cup blackberry brandy or liqueur**
- **4 Tbsps. cornstarch**
- **½ cup water**
- **1 package phyllo dough**
- **½ cup butter, melted**
- **Powdered sugar for dusting**
- **Frangelico Custard (recipe follows)**

Frangelico Custard
- **1/2 cup sugar**
- **4 Tbsps. cornstarch**
- **4 egg yolks**
- **2 1/2 cups whipping cream, scalded**
- **1/2 tsp. almond extract**
- **1/8 cup Frangelico liqueur**

In a saucepan bring the blackberries, sugar and brandy or liqueur to a boil. Mix the cornstarch with water and stir into the berries. Stir until the cornstarch is completely mixed with the berries. Cook until the berry mixture turns clear, then remove from the heat. Cool completely.

Brush the layers of phyllo dough with butter, repeating with the second and third layers. Spoon filling on the end of phyllo dough, roll twice, fold ends in and roll completely. Brush lightly with butter.

Bake seam side down at 350° for 15 to 20 minutes or until golden brown. Dust with powdered sugar. Top with Frangelico Custard.

Frangelico Custard

In the top of a double boiler, mix the sugar, cornstarch and egg yolks. Stir in the scalded cream until smooth. Cook and stir over hot water until custard is smooth and thickened. Remove from heat and stir in the almond extract and liqueur. Place in a bowl, cover with plastic wrap and chill before serving.

Jerry and Linda Evans
Jacksonville Inn Dinner House
Jacksonville, Oregon

Almond Peach Tart

Grind 1 cup of almonds in a food processor. Add the flour and ½ cup sugar, then add the butter, egg yolk and vanilla. Process with the on and off speed.

Press into the bottom and side of a tart or pie pan and cook at 375° until brown, about 20 minutes.

Spread the peach preserves over the cooked shell. Sprinkle with the remaining almond slices. Arrange the peaches over the nuts, sprinkle with remaining sugar and dot with butter.

Bake 35 minutes at 375°. Serve hot or cold.

Tom and Wendy Kreutner
Autumn Wind Vineyard
Newberg, Oregon

Serves 6
Preparation Time:
1¼ Hours
Pre-heat oven to 375°

1¼ cup sliced almonds
1 cup flour
½ cup + 3 Tbsps. sugar
½ cup butter
1 egg yolk, beaten
½ tsp. vanilla
2 Tbsps. peach preserves
1½ lbs. peaches, peeled, sliced
2 Tbsps. butter

Chocolate Hazelnut Tart

Serves 8 to 10
Preparation Time: One Hour
Pre-heat oven to 350°

- **¾ cup all-purpose flour**
- **6 Tbsps. powdered sugar**
- **¼ cup unsweetened cocoa**
- **¼ tsp. salt**
- **⅛ tsp. baking soda**
- **6 Tbsps. unsalted butter, cut into small cubes**
- **1 to 2 Tbsps. ice water**
- **1¼ cups hazelnuts, lightly toasted**
- **¼ cup each white, milk, and bittersweet chocolates, cut into 1-inch-sized chunks**
- **3 eggs**
- **1 cup light corn syrup**
- **½ cup sugar**
- **4 Tbsps. butter, melted**
- **1 tsp. vanilla extract**
- **Whipped cream, optional**

Prepare the chocolate pastry shell by sifting together the flour, sugar, cocoa, salt and baking soda in a large mixing bowl. Work in the butter until the mixture resembles a coarse meal. Add water 1 Tbsp. at a time until the mixture begins to form a dough. Wrap and chill for 30 minutes.

Roll the chilled pastry out, between parchment, to fit a tart pan. Line with foil and fill with beans or pastry weights. Bake 10 to 15 minutes at 350°. Cool.

Meanwhile, combine the hazelnuts and chocolate chunks. Set aside.

Beat the eggs slightly, then add the remaining filling ingredients. Blend well.

Fill the cooled tart shell with the nut and chocolate mixture. Pour the filling over the mixture. Bake the tart at 350° for 15 to 20 minutes or until the edges are set, but the center still quivers slightly. Cool.

Serve at room temperature with whipped cream.

Cory Schreiber
Wildwood Restaurant
Portland, Oregon

Ray's Boathouse Mixed Nut Tart

Serves 4
Preparation Time:
30 Minutes
Pre-heat oven to 425°

- **1½ cups flour**
- **¼ cup +2 tsps. sugar**
- **⅓ lb. butter, sliced**
- **4 egg yolks**
- **1 tsp. vanilla**
- **1 tsp. cold water**
- **2 cups walnuts**
- **¾ cup hazelnuts**
- **¾ cup sliced almonds**
- **½ cup brown sugar**
- **¼ cup honey**
- **2 tsp. white sugar**
- **¼ lb. butter**
- **¼ cup cream**
- **1 oz. bourbon**

In a large mixing bowl, sift together the flour and sugar. Add the butter. In a separate bowl, blend together the egg yolks, vanilla and water and add to the flour mixture.

Knead well. Roll into a circle 1-inch larger than the tart pan in diameter. Lightly press dough into the pan and trim so only ½-inch of the dough hangs over the top. Fold this edge over to the inside. Press with your fingers.

Bake at 425° for 8 to 10 minutes or until brown.

Roast the nuts until golden brown; be careful they don't burn.

Combine brown sugar, honey, 2 tsps. white sugar and butter in a heavy saucepan. Bring the mixture to a boil until caramelized. Add the cream and bourbon and stir well. Fold in the roasted nuts.

Pour into the baked tart shell and bake at 350° for 5 minutes. Cool on a wire rack.

Charles Ramseyer
Ray's Boathouse, Café & Catering
Seattle, Washington

Tiramisu

Serves 8
Preparation Time:
30 Minutes (Note Refrigeration Time)

- **1 cup sugar**
- **¾ cup brewed espresso**
- **¼ cup + 3 tsps. dark rum**
- **1½ cups heavy cream**
- **1 tsp. vanilla**
- **½ cup powdered sugar, sifted**
- **2 cups mascarpone**
- **26 ladyfingers**
- **Unsweetened cocoa powder**

Boil the sugar, espresso, and ¼ cup dark rum briefly until the sugar is dissolved. Set aside to cool.

In a mixing bowl, whip the cream with the 3 tsps. rum and the vanilla until soft peaks form. Set aside.

In a separate mixing bowl, slowly stir the powdered sugar into the mascarpone. Fold in the whipped cream.

Arrange a single layer of ladyfingers in the bottom of an 8-inch square glass dish. Use a pastry brush to soak the ladyfingers with one-third of the sugar and rum mixture. Evenly spread one-third of the mascarpone mixture over the ladyfingers. Sift a layer of about 2 Tbsps. cocoa over the mascarpone. Repeat the layering process twice more, finishing with a smooth layer of mascarpone. Do not add the final dusting of cocoa until just before serving.

Refrigerate for at least one hour, or up to 24 hours. Slice into 8 servings, arrange on dessert plates, dust with cocoa and serve.

David Machado
Pazzo Ristorante
Portland, Oregon

☆

Cabernet Truffles

Line a cookie sheet with waxed paper.

Bring the cream to a simmer in a heavy medium-size saucepan, then reduce to low and add the milk chocolate. Whisk until melted. Whisk in the butter and Cabernet.

Remove from the heat, cool and freeze at least 40 minutes or until firm enough to mound on a spoon. Drop the mixture onto a cookie sheet by the spoonful.

Freeze again until firm but pliable, about 30 minutes.

Roll each truffle in cocoa powder, then roll in the palm of your hands into a ball. Freeze again until firm.

Melt remaining dark chocolate with shortening, stirring until smooth. Dip each truffle and place on a clean waxed paper. Can be stored up to two weeks in refrigerator or freezer.

Pam and Joel Tefft
Tefft Cellars
Outlook, Washington

Serves 4
Preparation Time:
1½ Hours (Note Refrigeration Time)

- **½ cup whipping cream**
- **1½ cups milk chocolate, finely chopped**
- **½ cup butter**
- **¼ cup Cabernet**
- **1½ cups dark chocolate, finely chopped**
- **1 rounded tsp. grated orange peel, optional**
- **Unsweetened cocoa powder**
- **1 tsp. solid vegetable shortening**

Oregon
GOPA

BAY HOUSE

NORTHWEST CUISINE
5911 Southwest Highway 101
Lincoln City, Oregon
541-996-3222

The Bay House is a beautiful restaurant located on Siletz Bay on the Oregon Coast. Chef Greg Meixner takes great pride in creating fresh Northwest Cuisine in an innovative, continually evolving style that is very clean in flavor and presentation. Greg's philosophy is simple: Start with the highest quality ingredients and let the flavors come through naturally.

Menu highlights include Grilled Breast of Chicken with Carmelized Onions, Corn-Jalapeño Coulis and Roasted Potatoes; Fresh Halibut dusted with Parmesan, baked and served with a Lemon Béchamel Sauce; and Grilled Prawns and Soba Noodles with Spicy Asian Vegetables and Yellow Curry Sauce.

Open Nightly for Dinner at 5:30 PM
AVERAGE DINNER FOR TWO: $70

CANYON WAY RESTAURANT AND BOOKSTORE

1216 Southwest Canyon Way
Newport, Oregon
541-265-8319

The combination bookstore and restaurant offers a large luncheon and dinner menu, plus scores of specials by Chef Mike Downing.

The philosophy here is to use only the freshest ingredients. All of the soups, sauces, dressings and chowders are homemade. Chef Downing oversees the making of pasta, bakes fresh bread daily for every meal, and prepares all the desserts and pastries in-house.

Menu specialties include Dungeness Crab Cakes mixed with herbs and bread crumbs, grilled in butter and served with homemade Creole mayonnaise and Angel Hair Onion Rings, and Chicken Tuscany, which is marinated with olive oil, lemon, rosemary and garlic, then char-grilled and topped with a sun-dried tomato pesto. Pasta highlights include the Ginger Garlic Shrimp Pasta, sautéed with Bell Peppers, Mushrooms and Onions in an Oriental Sauce and the Seafood Marinara Pasta in a homemade Italian Tomato Sauce.

Open for Lunch Monday–Saturday 11AM–3PM
Dinner Tuesday–Saturday 5PM–9PM
AVERAGE DINNER FOR TWO: $75

Chateaulin Restaurant and Wine Shoppe

FRENCH CUISINE
50 East Main
Ashland, Oregon
541-482-2264

Step through the doors and enter a romantic café reminiscent of New York's upper west side. Exposed brick walls hung with copper kettles and old champagne bottles give the restaurant a casually elegant appearance that is accented by lace curtains, burgundy table cloths and dark wood furnishings.

Located right next door to the Oregon Shakespeare Festival, Chateaulin has been regarded as one of the best restaurants in the Rogue Valley since it first opened in 1973. Chef/Owner David Taub has a passion to buy the freshest, best ingredients available, and prepare them in a simple, colorful, uncluttered style.

Entrées follow culinary trends that include pan-roasted Loin of Oregon Lamb with a sauce of red wine, demi-glaze, fresh thyme, shallots and roasted garlic. The vegetarian Crepes Florentine are made with fresh spinach, shallots, portobello mushrooms, and Willamette Valley goat cheese. The delicate butterflied shrimp is served in a subtle sauce of sherry, cream, tomato and brandy.

The restaurant's wine list is impressive and features hundreds of premium wines from around the world, with a distinct emphasis on hard-to-find wines from some of the best small vineyards in the Pacific Northwest.

Open Daily for Dinner, 5:30PM–9PM
AVERAGE DINNER FOR TWO: $70

CHEZ JEANNETTE

FRENCH CUISINE
7150 Old Highway 101
Gleneden Beach, Oregon
503-764-3434

Nestled in the woods of Gleneden Beach lies a quaint little 1920s cottage called Chez Jeannette. Thick branches curl around the roof and walls of this homey stone-fronted structure resting snugly against a vine-covered hill. A small colorful front garden, perfect for a stroll, with flower boxes lining the windows, only serves to make the cottage more magical.

Dark and ornate wallpaper, a crackling fireplace illuminating the softly lit rooms and walls, partially covered with stone and beamed ceilings make this look like the fairy tale Hansel & Gretel Cottage.

Every night there are different seafood specials as well as pasta du jour. Entrées include Veal Medallions sautéed and served with a sauce of Dijon Mustard and Shiitake Mushrooms finished with a Brandy Demi-Glaze and Boneless Breast of Chicken, sautéed in olive oil, and served with a sauce of golden raisins, fresh thyme, rosemary, pine nuts and veal stock. The nightly selection of homemade desserts is as tempting as the rest of the meal at Chez Jeannette.

Open for Dinner Monday–Sunday 5:30PM–10PM
AVERAGE DINNER FOR TWO: $80

GENOA

NORTHERN ITALIAN CUISINE
2832 Southeast Belmont Street
Portland, Oregon
503-238-1464

Genoa recently celebrated twenty-five years of serving prix fixe Northern Italian dinners. Early arrivals are escorted into the comfortable sitting room furnished with stuffed chairs to encourage you to blind-taste several varieties of wines and choose a favorite.

The dinners, which are imaginative yet traditional, are based on the regional cuisines of Italy. The setting is warm and comfortable, in keeping with the belief that dinner with good food is both festive and a time for conversation and relaxation. The restaurant is simple, with dark colors and round tables. Not too fancy, but the service is unsurpassed.

The menu changes weekly but the dishes will dazzle. Some highlights include Agnolotti di Zuca: tender envelopes of fresh egg pasta filled with a mixture of sweetmeat squash, sweet potatoes, crushed amaretti cookies, Parmesan cheese and a touch of nutmeg, served with butter and garnished with fried sage leaves. The fresh Kamilche Bay mussels, wonderfully briny and tasting of the sea, are skewered with pancetta and parboiled leeks, lightly grilled and served with lemon.

Desserts arrive on a tray laden with a legendary selection of extravagant chocolate and nut tortes, caramelized tarts of apples and pears, liqueur-infused tarts, creamy custards, gelati and sorbetti. Fresh seasonal fruit completes the meal.

Open for Dinner Monday–Saturday 5:30PM–9:30PM
AVERAGE DINNER FOR TWO: $100 (four-course prix fixe)

JARBOE'S IN MANZANITA

137 Laneda Avenue
Manzanita, Oregon
503-368-5113

ocated in a cozy remodeled cottage, Jarboe's is modestly decorated with simple furnishings. Danish-born chef/owner Klaus Monberg is responsible for the creative and frequently changing menu.

Velvety soups and bisques featuring fresh seafood take on new textures and flavors in his kitchen. Menu highlights include Mesquite-Broiled Meats, Fowl and Seafood as well as Poached Pears with Crème Anglaise and an Almond-Crusted Chocolate Cake.

Open for Dinner Thursday–Monday 5:30–9:30PM
AVERAGE DINNER FOR TWO: $80

L'AUBERGE

FRENCH CUISINE
2601 Northwest Vaughn Street
Portland, Oregon
503-223-3302

L'Auberge is a relaxing retreat offering a formal dining room and full-service bar in addition to al fresco dining on the deck in the summer months.

For over 25 years, L'Auberge has been nationally recognized for devotion to serious, imaginative food while drawing upon traditional and contemporary French concepts of preparation.

Serving dinner every evening, prix fixe meals and a la carte dining are enjoyed in an intimate setting of candlelight and fireplaces.

Sample highlights include Curried Squid Stew with Tomatoes, Garlic and Olives, Roasted Rack of Lamb with a Roasted Garlic Cake and Oregano Tapenade Sauce, Grilled Marinated Prawns with Curry Polenta and Fresh Mangos and a Bittersweet Chocolate Terrine with Dark Cherries in a Spiced Pinot Noir Sauce.

Open for Dinner Monday–Saturday 5:30PM–9PM
AVERAGE DINNER FOR TWO: $70

Pazzo Ristorante

NORTHERN ITALIAN CUISINE
627 Southwest Washington
Portland, Oregon
503-228-1212

Located on the corner of Broadway and Washington Street, Pazzo Ristorante is one of Portland's most popular restaurants, where Italian friendliness, a contemporary setting merge. Pazzo features Northern Italian cuisine served in a high-energy atmosphere.

Coffered ceilings, Italian marble floors, dark wood and warm lighting add to the atmosphere. The walls above the bar are decorated with garlands of garlic, dried peppers, sausages and herbs. Large picture windows line two sides of the restaurant, providing views for guests seated around tables draped in red-checkered cloths.

The kitchen is fully visible from the dining room and features a large wood-burning pizza oven and a hardwood-fired grill. The menu features fresh ingredients prepared in unusual combinations such as Pasta Stuffed with Butternut Squash in a Hazelnut Marsala Butter, Grilled Venison Chops with Saffron Risotto Cakes and Dried Cherry Grappa Sauce, and Grilled Stuffed Pork Chops with Garlic Mashed Potatoes in a Pinenut and Currant Sauce.

Open for Breakfast Monday–Sunday 8AM–10:30AM
Lunch Monday–Saturday 11:30AM–2:30PM
Dinner Monday–Sunday 5PM–10PM
AVERAGE DINNER FOR TWO: $85

3 Doors Down

ITALIAN AND PACIFIC CUISINE
1429 Southeast 37th Avenue
Portland, Oregon
503-236-6886

Named for the fact that this restaurant is three doors down from the Hawthorne District, the 3 Doors Down is a blend of Italian cuisine with a touch of Pacific Northwest.

The decor is eccentric: white tables and candles with an industrial concrete floor. The café is housed in a simple storefront, but there are some striking touches.

The dining room walls are bathed in supersaturated colors such as deep Prussian blue and terra-cotta, while the stepped-down wall fronting the open kitchen is sunflower yellow.

The menu changes regularly, but be sure to try the bountiful Seafood Fra Diavolo, Parmesan-laced Steamed Clams, and the Pasta Studded with Copper River Salmon. Finish with the intense Chocolate Torte or the dauntingly rich Cheesecake.

Open for Dinner Tuesday–Sunday 5PM–10PM
AVERAGE DINNER FOR TWO: $50

WILDWOOD RESTAURANT

PACIFIC NORTHWEST CUISINE
1221 Northwest 21st Avenue
Portland, Orego
503-248-9663n

Wildwood is the place to go if you are in the mood for refined Pacific Northwest cuisine. It has one of the nicest patios for outdoor dining in the Portland area. Terrazzo counters, wood floors and Douglas Fir tables contribute to the casual yet contemporary atmosphere. A glass and ceramic mural featuring a tribute to Portland natives by a local artist greets patrons upon entry. The clean and modern design is both stylish and comfortable.

Chef/owner Cory Schreiber, a Portland native, named the restaurant for a popular hiking trail in nearby Forest Park. In homage to the spirit of the Pacific Northwest, Cory stocks up on local products, then artfully combines them to create delicious, uncomplicated dishes.

The menu is market-driven, featuring fresh seasonal ingredients utilizing local farms and purveyors, a diversity of meats, seafood, pizzas, pastas, vegetables, salads and other savories.

Among some of the must-try entrées are the Oregon Rabbit with Pancetta-Wrapped Pear and Wild Mushrooms, and Cornmeal-Crust Pizzas.

The wine list reflects Wildwood's northwestern exposure in an outstanding selection of regional bottlings, including many produced by small wineries whose vintages are rarely seen in other parts of the country.

Open for Lunch Monday–Saturday 11:30AM–2:30PM
Dinner Monday–Saturday 5:30 PM–10PM
Sunday Brunch 10AM–2PM
Family Style Supper Sunday 5 PM–9:30PM
AVERAGE DINNER FOR TWO: $80

Chanticleer Inn

120 Gresham Street
Ashland, Oregon 97520
541-482-1919
800-898-1950
ROOM RATES: $69–$160

Built in the 1920s, the Chanticleer Inn was one of the first bed and breakfast establishments in Ashland reflecting the European country feeling. The Inn strives to be a home-away-from-home, offering a comfortable firelit living room, well-stocked bookshelves, a cookie jar that is never empty, and an open invitation to raid the kitchen for late night snacks. Guests can curl up in the comfy chairs in the spacious living room while warming their toes by the open-hearth fireplace. Innkeeper Pebby Kuan is an avid walker who advises guests to park their cars out back and not to start them again until they leave.

Filled with elegant antiques, each of the six named guest rooms has a unique personality. Each room has a private bath. The Maître Room is located on the main floor with a queen-size antique brass bed and French windows with views of the garden and mountains. Some rooms overlook the Bear Creek Valley and Cascades foothills while others open onto the garden patio that is lined with rose bushes, lilies, and brilliantly colored perennials. Guest rooms are furnished with fluffy comforters, Persian carpets, fresh flowers, imported soaps and lotions, firm beds, good reading lamps, current magazines and the scripts of all plays being performed at the nearby Shakespeare Festival only four blocks away.

Breakfast is served daily in the sun-filled dining room, offering tempting treats such as Ricotta Pancakes, Crab Quiche and Apple and Turkey sausages. Guests can also have breakfast delivered to their rooms and enjoy the calm of the Chanticleer Inn.

Columbia Gorge Hotel

4000 Westcliff Drive
Hood River, Oregon 97031
541-386-5566
ROOM RATES: $150–$270

Lumber baron Simon Benson built the Columbia Gorge Hotel in 1921, and throughout the years, it has been a favorite with honeymooners and tourists. The spacious lobby-lounge is much the same as it was a half century ago, with its stunning structure, private windows on the Wah-Gwin-Gwin Falls, which plunges 200 feet down into the Columbia River, and a colorful past including visits from Rudolph Valentino.

Impressive and high-ceilinged but not cavernlike, the room has tall velvet-draped windows and groupings of comfortable sofas, chairs and tables well placed for tea, cocktails, conversation or enjoying the nightly piano music. Each guest room has its own color scheme and small bath with a basket of scented soaps and bath oils. The package deals are the most fun: murder mystery weekends, seven-course winemaker dinners, fly-fishing in the mountains, or eco-tours of the gorge are among some of the best.

Chef Britt Unkerfer created a unique menu that offers Lobster Strudel with Lobster Cream Sauce, Sautéed Salmon with Red Pepper Coulis and Fennel Slaw, and Wilted Spinach Salad with Smoked Duck and Bacon. Fine dining and entertainment are the rule at the Columbia Gorge Hotel.

HERON HAUS BED & BREAKFAST

2545 Northwest Westover Road
Portland, Oregon 97210
503-274-1846
ROOM RATES: $135–$250

Sitting high on the western hills of Portland, the Heron Haus is an elegant, ivy-covered, three-story 1904 English Tudor house. Innkeeper Julie Keppeler makes the inn a warm and friendly place by covering the walls with family photos and family treasures. Expansive views of mountains and the city, fruit trees in the lower garden, old ballast stones from sailing ships, leaded glass windows and intricate ceiling moldings create warmth and harmony throughout the three-story home. The views from the living room, library and sun room are of the city and Mount St. Helen's.

Julie's many years in Hawaii are reflected in the overall feeling of airiness and light of the inn, but also in the names of the rooms. With six guest rooms in shades of blue, lavender and rose, guests will find one that fits their needs and desires. The Ko (sugar) room, located on the second floor, has two sitting rooms, and the Mahina (moonlight) room, located on the third floor, offers incredible views of Mount Hood and Mount St. Helen's. The bathrooms each have a special feature such as a shower with seven showerheads and a spa on a windowed porch with a view of the city.

A pastry-laden breakfast is served daily, and Julie recommends several outstanding local, nearby places for lunch and dinner.

Hood River Hotel

102 Oak Street
Hood River, Oregon 97031
541-386-1900
800-386-1859
ROOM RATES: $49–$145

The oldest hotel in its town, the Hood River Hotel is a truly romantic getaway. Even though centrally located in the heart of town, guests feel as if they have taken a step back in time when they arrive at this fully restored vintage hotel. Guests can enjoy espressos or after-dinner drinks in front of the lobby fireplace or at an outside table while listening to jazz, blues or country music.

Fresh flowers, fireside seating and a conscientious staff ensure a pleasurable stay. Each of the 41 rooms and suites have different and individualized antique reproductions. Some of the rooms come with four-poster, sleigh or brass beds, pedestal sinks, and plenty of floral chintz. Most of the rooms have a fireplace or a whirlpool bath where guests can unwind after a long day of sightseeing. Guests can enjoy year-round snow skiing on Mount Hood, golfing, river rafting, horseback riding, and windsurfing on the Columbia River.

Pasquale's Ristorante offers a combination of Italian and Pacific Northwest cuisines, serving breakfast, lunch and dinner. The emphasis is on local fruits and fish.

Hudson House Bed & Breakfast Inn

37700 U.S. Highway 101 South
Cloverdale, Oregon 97112
503-392-3533
ROOM RATES: $60–$80

Built in 1906, Hudson House Bed & Breakfast Inn was a Victorian farmhouse owned by Clyde Hudson, a locally known photographer who documented the growth of the Cloverdale area and whose work is on display at the inn. Perched on a bluff in the middle of nowhere, it evokes memories of Grandma's house. Innkeepers Richard and Judy Shinton paid careful attention to the tiny details when restoring the inn because their wish was to make the inn feel as if it was transplanted from the turn of the century. This inn is a relaxing getaway from the stresses of everyday life, and whether you are celebrating a special occasion or just in need of a mini-vacation, the Hudson House will make you feel pampered and relaxed.

The four guest rooms are named after Richard and Judy's grandmothers and include personal items from their lives. They are all decorated in an early-century country style and overlook forested hillsides surrounding the pastoral Nestucca River valley. The Matilda Room is a bright and airy room with two antique iron double beds with blue and yellow quilts facing the orchard and garden. The Mary Ester Suite has a spacious bedroom, sitting room and private porch overlooking Nestucca Valley pastures and the Coast Range done in pinks, burgundies and blues.

A hearty breakfast starts your day off right. It includes some unusual treats such as British bangers (sausage), Dutch pancakes, and homemade Wholly cow cereal. Arriving back at the inn after a long day's adventure, guests find coffee, tea and homemade goodies waiting for them.

JACKSONVILLE INN

175 East California Street
P.O. Box 359
Jacksonville, Oregon 97530
541-899-1900
800-321-9344
ROOM RATES: $80–$225

The Jacksonville Inn is housed in one of Gold Rush Jacksonville's early permanent buildings and perpetuates the nostalgic romance of the era. It was the first two-story brick building raised in 1861 and served as several different businesses, including a bank, hardware store, furniture repair shop, and professional offices before becoming the Jacksonville Inn.

Guests enjoy the little knick-knacks that make this inn feel like a home. Patchwork quilts on the beds and brickwork on the walls create a home-and-hearth feeling for the guests. Filled with authentic western antiques, the eight guest rooms have queen-sized beds and private bathrooms. Some of the rooms have brass bedstead, while some have oak with five-foot high headboards. All the rooms have air-conditioning. The three guest cottages, located one and a half blocks away from the Inn, are furnished with canopied king sized beds, Jacuzzis, steam showers, full entertainment centers, and fireplaces.

Delectable cuisine demands the diner to savor every mouthful to the fullest. Executive Chef Diane Menzie creates a full realm of continental cuisine: steak, pasta, plus health-minded low-cholesterol and vegetarian fare. The wine cellar is stocked with over 1,500 wines to meet even the most discriminating connoisseur's desires.

The Lion and The Rose Victorian Bed and Breakfast

1810 North East 15th
Portland, Oregon 97212
503-287-9245
800-955-1647
Room Rates: $85–150

Recently becoming a designated landmark, The Lion and The Rose is a one-of-a-kind 1906 Queen Anne house in Portland's historical Irvington District. Displaying the influences of English and medieval Architecture that were part of the revival influence of the era, The Lion and The Rose is a beautiful building.

The seven guest rooms are each warm and inviting in their own way. The Lavonna Room is the most popular and romantic. With a unique round room setting in shades of lavender and green, the king-sized iron bed is complemented by a beautiful backdrop draped canopy. In shades of pink and white, the Escapade Room has a king-sized canopy bed draped in yards of sheer organza. The Starina Room is done in dark rich shades of green, rust and gold that warm you the minute you step in. The focal point of this room is the circa-1860 high-back Edwardian bed and its matching accessories. Each of the other four have their own color schemes and characteristics that make them unique.

Breakfast is served in the dining room and guests are within walking distance of many fine restaurants, shops and boutiques.

Mount Ashland Inn

550 Mount Ashland Road
Ashland, Oregon 97520
541-482-8707
800-830-8707
Room Rates: $95–$145

Nestled in the middle of tall evergreens, the Mount Ashland Inn is a four-floor log and frame structure, built over 3 years, opening on Christmas Eve in 1987. The living room has a large stone fireplace that is perfect for sipping hot cocoa in front of, game tables, and reading area. The dining room offers views of the Cascade Mountains including the majestic Mount Shasta. Recently added facilities include an outdoor spa and sauna surrounded by large white fir trees. This is truly an Inn for all seasons. With cross-country trails outside the front door and the downhill slopes of Mount Ashland a few miles away, guests can take in the best of winter. In the summer, hikers can enjoy the panoramic views along the Pacific Crest Trail. But for the travelers who are in the mood to just relax at the inn, the scenery is just as beautiful from the rooms.

The inn has five guest rooms and suites. Each room has a private bath and is individually decorated from the bed linen to the hand-crafted furniture. The Cottonwood Room has a romantic queen bed with a handpainted antique headboard and a handmade quilt, and incredible views of unspoiled forest. The Sky Lakes Suite is perfect for a honeymoon. With a whirlpool-for-two, a trickling rock waterfall, views of Mount Shasta and McLoughlin, king-sized bed with handmade quilt and private entrance, the lovely room is a newlywed couple's dream.

The Inn offers a hearty breakfast to satisfy any mountain of an appetite. Some of the specialties include Orange French Toast, Apple-Walnut Whole-Wheat Pancakes and Shrimp Quiche.

Ponderosa Cattle Company Guest Ranch

60660 Bobiat Road
Bend, Oregon 97702
541-542-2403
800-331-1012
ROOM RATES: $80–100 per day (Special package rates available)

In the Silvies Valley of Eastern Oregon, situated on 120,000 acres, the Ponderosa Guest Ranch is an authentic working cattle ranch with over 3000 head of cattle and elk. Guests learn to do real ranch work including driving cattle to mountain pastures, sorting, branding, vaccinating, helping during calving, gathering, scattering and moving cattle from pasture to pasture.

During the winter months, guests can enjoy romantic horse-drawn sleigh rides, cross-country skiing and snowmobiling. Weather permitting, guests can also enjoy hiking, fishing or a jump in the old swimming hole. The 7,000 square-foot log lodge houses the dining room, bar-lounge, library, sitting room, gift shop, and a fabulous view of the valley. The lodge is the perfect place for relaxing or dancing after a day on the trail. The Ponderosa is the kind of place where a vacation can turn into a defining moment.

The eight log guest cabins are divided into three separate units, each including two double beds and a full bathroom. Guests can enjoy beautiful sunsets from their cabin's covered porch.

You are guaranteed to work up an appetite. Meals are eaten family-style in the main lodge, or from the chuckwagon. And when the chow bell rings, you can bet it'll be good 'home cookin'.

RIVERPLACE HOTEL

1510 Southwest Harbor Way
Portland, Oregon 97201
503-228-3233
800-227-1333
Room Rates: $185–$700

Nestled on the waterfront in the heart of the Portland downtown business district, the RiverPlace Hotel gives the feeling of a true urban resort. The elegantly furnished rooms and suites offer spectacular views of Portland's waterfront, the downtown skyline and the RiverPlace marina. Guests enjoy walking along the paved path that leads from the hotel front door to the heart of downtown Portland.

The hotel has over 70 rooms. Most are done in post modern colors, with televisions hidden in armoires and plush furnishings. The rooms have views of the Willamette River, the park lawns or the downtown cityscape.

Guests can enjoy breakfast, lunch, dinner or Sunday brunch in the elegant Esplanade Restaurant overlooking the Willamette River. Executive Chef John Zenger's creations are mouth-watering delights. Some of the specialties offered are a Esplanade Salad with Warm Brie Dressing and the Pacific Halibut and Fresh Chanterelles Simmered in Vietnamese-Style Caramel Sauce among others.

STEPHANIE INN

2740 South Pacific Street
Cannon Beach, Oregon 97110
503-436-2221
800-633-3466
Room Rates: $129–$369

The Stephanie Inn is located on Cannon Beach and offers spectacular views of the Pacific Ocean and misty coastal mountains. Built in 1993, the inn is a blend of elegance, charm and quiet seclusion creating an enchanting hideaway. Built of cedar and river rock, the inn seems to blend into the surroundings as if it sprang naturally from the earth. The staff is attentive, but not intrusive. The inn offers several packages for guests including a Honeymoon, Anniversary, Birthday and Romance Package where a bottle of champagne awaits guests in their rooms.

The 46 beautifully furnished rooms all have gas fireplaces and Jacuzzi tubs. The typical oceanfront room has a four poster bed, wingback chairs and couch, and entertainment center. The Ocean Front Corner Suite is a two-bedroom suite with a bathroom featuring a corner Jacuzzi and shower.

The Chart Room restaurant is an intimate and romantic setting for meals. Breakfast is a delight, featuring entrées such as Grand Marnier French Toast. Dinners are available for guests at a prix fixe.

Cannon Beach, Oregon

ASHLAND VINEYARDS & WINERY

2775 East Main Street
Ashland, Oregon 97520
541-488-0088
800-503-WINE
Tasting room

Similar in climate to the Bordeaux region of France, this part of southern Oregon's Rogue Valley is home to Ashland Vineyards, owned by Phil and Kathy Kodak. Encompassing 120 acres, it is the largest in this part of the state.

A greenhouse and nursery are found on the estate where grape starts are propagated. After a visit to the tasting room, the panoramic mountain views that surround the ponds and picnic areas beckon visitors as a site to enjoy lunch, along with a glass of their award-winning Cabernet, Merlot, Sauvignon Blanc or Chardonnay.

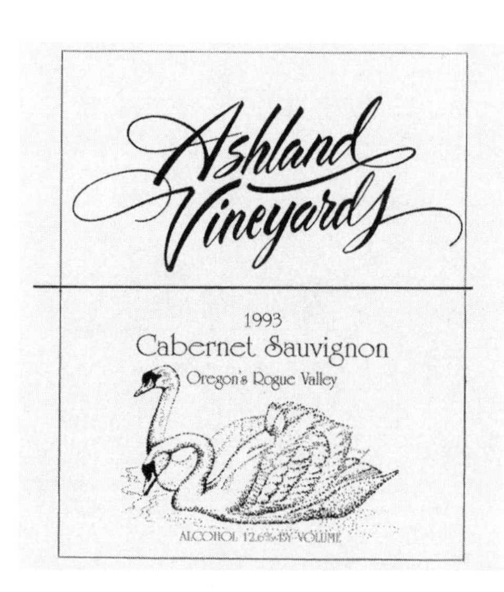

AUTUMN WIND VINEYARD

15225 Northeast North Valley Road
Newberg, Oregon 97132
503-538-6931
Open Weekends for Wine Tasting & Tours: Noon–5PM

Located in the North Chehalem Valley in the heart of Yamhill County's wine country, Tom and Wendy Kreutner chose the name Autumn Wind for their winery to suggest the warmth, color and feel of the fall grape harvest in Oregon. This is that magic time when the warm winds blow through the vineyard and the grape leaves turn a spectacular gold and red, with newly picked grapes being wondrously transformed into white and red wines.

The Kreutners began clearing cherry trees in 1984 to make way for Chardonnay, Pinot Noir, Sauvignon Blanc, Pinot Gris and Muller-Thurgau. They concentrate on only a few varieties, so that they could put all their efforts into producing truly fine wines.

Bethel Heights Vineyards

6060 Bethel Heights Road Northwest
Salem, Oregon 97304
503-581-2262
Tasting Room: Tuesday–Sunday 11AM–5PM June–August
Saturday & Sunday 11AM–5PM March–May & September–December 24
Closed December 25–March

Bethel Heights Vineyard, with a commanding view of Mount Jefferson and Spring Valley, was one of the earliest vineyards planted in the Eola Hills.

Since 1977, it has been establishing its reputation for Pinot Noir and Chardonnay. Located 12 miles northwest of Salem in the central Willamette Valley, the winery stands on the site of an apple orchard, pioneered by nineteenth-century settlers, with a church and cemetery from the same period nearby.

Cooper Mountain Vineyards

9480 Southwest Grabhorn Road
Beaverton, Oregon 97007
503-649-0027
Tasting Room Open Weekends Noon–5PM

Perched on the top of an extinct volcano overlooking the Tualatin River Valley, a breathtaking view sweeps from the Cooper Mountain Vineyard vantage point, 15 miles southwest of Portland.

The vineyard sells the majority of the grapes produced, allowing the winery to estate bottle only small amounts of premium Pinot Noir, Chardonnay and Pinot Gris.

Owners Bob and Corinne Gross are dedicated to the concept of 100% estate grown and produced wine, exercising direct control of all the decisions relating to the final quality of the wine, from pruning in the field to aging in the bottle.

Duck Pond Cellars

23145 Highway 99 West
P.O. Box 429
Dundee, Oregon 97115
503-538-3199
Tasting Room: Open Daily 11AM–5PM

The Fries family worked together to plant their own vineyard in 1986, opening the winery with a year-round tasting room 7 years later. Today it is still a family-run winery in the truest sense, with all five members of the Fries family being active in the operation, and with son, Greg, as winemaker.

The family's efforts are dedicated to producing premium quality wines at affordable prices. So far, from the Willamette Valley holdings, their focus has been on Pinot Noir and Chardonnay and will shortly include an Estate Grown Pinot Gris. The Waluke Slope in Washington State will also be producing Merlot and Cabernet under the Duck Pond label.

In Dundee, the winery's intimate size allows for greater flexibility in the harvesting, fermenting and aging of the wines and permits careful nurturing of each vintage, allowing Duck Pond to deliver an excellent wine at an affordable price.

Elk Cove Vineyards

27751 Northwest Olson Road
Gaston, Oregon 97119
503-985-7760
Tasting room: Daily 11AM–5PM

In the springtime, it's not unusual to sight the elk that gave the vineyard its name. They are at home here, wandering through the steep slopes surrounding this 24-acre vineyard, owned by Joe and Patricia Campbell some 30 miles southwest of Portland.

The Campbells believe that it was an outstanding site that they chose back in 1976 to cultivate for the planting of a selection of individual vines from their older Estate Reserve field. Extracting a world-class Pinot Noir was the objective.

The fruits of their efforts were later harvested in 1989 with the debut of their 1989 La Boheme, a Pinot Noir destined to take the gold at the San Francisco Wine Competition—and confirming the Campbells' belief.

Erath Vineyards

9009 Northeast Worden Hill Road
P.O. Box 667
Dundee, Oregon 97115
503-538-3318
Open Daily for Tasting: 11AM–5PM
Tours: By Appointment

According to winemaker Dick Erath, it was an act of faith to grow wine grapes over 20 years ago in Oregon. Back then, it was questionable whether or not vinifera quality grapes could be grown there, much less making consistently good wine from them.

With the planting of Erath Vineyards in 1967, Dick Erath proved to himself (and a company of critics) that wine grapes could be grown as bountifully as the area's peaches, plums and cherries.

Believing that an area that had become known for their premium Pinot Noirs could also be an outstanding source for Chardonnay, Erath rallied to plant Dijon clones, known for their small berries and clusters that add characteristic dimension and intensity—and further renown for this region's white varietals.

FLERCHINGER VINEYARDS

4200 Post Canyon Drive
Hood River Valley, Oregon 97031
541-386-2882
800-516-8710
Open Daily For Wine Tasting 11AM–5PM

The Flerchinger Vineyard and Winery sits lazily in the bottom of a hammock of orchards, rivers and old-growth forests supported by the year- round snow-capped Mount Hoodto the south and majestic Mount Adams to the north. The Columbia River and four large tributaries are nearby, providing some of the world's finest freshwater fishing and water sports.

The grounds around the winery are complemented by numerous free-standing rock walls, oak trees and wild flowers, as well as quail and pheasant.

The covered patio, lawn and tasting room enjoy frequent use for catered parties and dances. The winery also celebrates a Blossom and Harvest Festival that is open to the public each year and features special tasting menus.

Along with Cabernet Sauvignon, Merlot, and Chardonnay, Flerchinger is also known for their dry style of Riesling.

HENRY ESTATE

687 Hubbard Creek Road
Umpqua, Oregon 97486
541-459-5120
Tasting room: Daily 11AM–5PM

Returning after 13 years to the family homestead in the heart of the Umpqua Valley after a career in aeronautical engineering, Scott Henry was ready to come back to the land. Enlisting long-time friend Gino Zepponi as a winemaking consultant, they decided on the warm, dry Umpqua Valley.

Known for its multitude of soil geographies as the most diversified growing region in the state, the Henry Estate Winery was built in 1978. Here, Scott Henry perfected the vertical trellis that now carries his name, a trellising system that is used to optimize the maturity of grapes in wine-producing regions all over the world.

The Henry Estate Winery continues to be one of the state's oldest and most prestigious producers of Pinot Noir and Chardonnay.

MONTINORE VINEYARDS

3663 Southwest Dilley Road
P.O. Box 650
Forest Grove, Oregon 97116
503-359-5012
Tasting Room: Open Daily Noon–5PM

Nestled in the gentle hills of Oregon's fertile Willamette River Valley, Montinore Vineyards sits on a unique parcel of land where the growing conditions for wine grapes are the very same as are found in the Burgundy region of France.

Montinore's name is a shortened version of "Montana-in-Oregon". Near the turn of the century, John Forbis moved from Montana to purchase part of the 711 acres of the property and christened it with that sentiment in mind.

Begun in 1982, the estate actually owes its birth to the explosive devastation of Mount St. Helens in 1980. The eruption that destroyed the vegetable and fruit crops of the area later effected the potential for production of world-class grape varieties.

Oak Knoll Winery

29700 Southwest Burkhalter Road
Hillsboro, Oregon 97123
503-648-8198
Open Daily for Tours & Tasting Noon–5PM

ounded in 1970, Oak Knoll Winery is one of the oldest wineries in the state. Owned and operated by the Vuylsteke family, the picturesque winery is housed in an old dairy, with the hollow tile construction providing perfect cellar temperature.

The family began making fruit wines early on, largely because of the scarcity of wine grapes at that time. The Vuylstekes then began buying grapes from a large stable of dedicated growers from all over the Willamette Valley.

From this practice they found that by blending the grapes that were the product of a variety of soil and climactic conditions from all over the valley, the resulting wines were of a very intricate structure with subtle nuances.

By making small, usually two-barrel experimental batches of wine from grapes of various locations, the flavors were found to differ remarkably—lending winemaker Steve Vuylsteke a flavor palette from which intricate wines could be crafted, as he describes it, "the sum of which is greater than the parts."

TYEE WINE CELLARS

26355 Greenberry Road
Corvallis, Oregon 97333
503-753-8754
Open Weekends for Tasting: Noon–5PM

Located on the scenic 460-acre Century Farm that was established by the Buchanan family in 1885, this winery offers visitors the experience of tasting fine wine while taking a look back in history.

Visitors are invited to guide themselves on a walking tour and stroll through canopies of oaks and hazelnut orchards and past beaver ponds to find the perfect picnic spot during the months of May through September.

Choosing the Northwest Native American word for "chief" or the "best," owners Barney Watson, Nola Mosier and Dave and Margy Buchanan feel that the name also applies to their limited production of premium varietal wines.

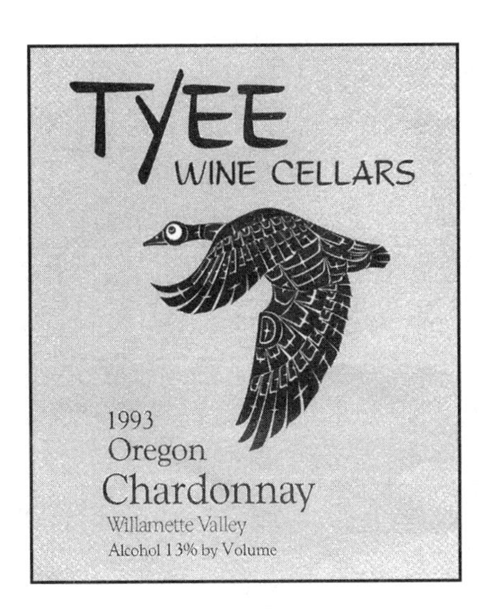

WEISINGER'S OF ASHLAND VINEYARD AND WINERY

3150 Siskiyou Boulevard
Ashland, Oregon 97520
541-488-5989
Tasting room: Wednesday–Sunday 11AM–5PM

On a hill overlooking the valley, Weisinger's of Ashland is a family-operated winery and 6-acre vineyard located in the heart of Oregon's Rogue Valley Appellation. Tasting and tours are conducted at the tasting room and gift shop, where gourmet food items, gifts for wine enthusiasts and picnicking supplies are featured, along with a well-stocked deli-case and picnic area.

Winemaker John Weisinger specializes in premium European-style wines such as an Alsatian-style Gewürtzraminer and their internationally awarded Semillon-Chardonnay blend. Other unique blends include the "Petite Pompadour" in the Bordeaux style and "Mescolare," an Italian-inspired wine.

Washington
GOPA

AL BOCCALINO RISTORANTE

ITALIAN CUISINE
1 Yesler Way
Seattle, Washington
206-622-7688

Nestled inside a triangular brick building at the foot of the oldest and most infamous street in Seattle, the Al Boccalino Ristorante has carved itself into the totem pole of an historic Seattle neighborhood by introducing a sophisticated and classical Italian cuisine to modern urban diners.

Located on the original site of Henry Yelser's sawmill, Seattle's first sawmill, the bricks are offset by the cream walls, green carpeting and high archways giving the restaurant a feeling of an old world home.

Al Boccalino received immediate and unexpected acclaim after opening in 1989, combining the simple and rustic nature of southern Italian cooking with the complexity and richness of northern Italian cooking and bravely offering an all-Italian wine list. The Italian fare has many highlights including the Roasted Quail with Prosciutto, Lamb with a Tarragon Mustard Sauce, and Pears Poached in Wine.

Open Daily for Dinner
AVERAGE DINNER FOR TWO: $80

Bay Café

ECLECTIC INTERNATIONAL CUISINE
Lopez Town
Lopez Island, Washington
360-468-3700

This small and cheery café is located on one of the most remote islands of the Pacific Northwest regions. From the channel, sailors can see the weather-washed sign on the front of the building accented by the imposing figure of a solitary great blue heron.

During the first three years in business, the ethnic cuisine changed weekly. Slowly but surely, the inventiveness paid off as ethnic culinary experiences fused into a hybrid menu that changes seasonally. Operating a restaurant on a remote island offers unique challenges including missed ferries and planes unable to land. Improvisation is a lesson quickly learned.

The dishes are a mixture of ethnic cuisines from all over the world. Using locally cultivated shiitake mushrooms in a Spanish tapenade or utilizing Chinese eggroll wrappers to make Italian ravioli make the usual fare memorable.

Open for Dinner From 5:30PM; Closed Tuesday
AVERAGE DINNER FOR TWO: $40

CHEZ SHEA

NORTHWEST CUISINE
94 Pike Street, Suite 34
Seattle, Washington
206-467-9990

The perfect setting for a romantic dinner, Chez Shea is a quiet, dark and very intimate fine restaurant in Seattle with views across Puget Sound to the Olympic Mountains. The candlelight throws shadows across the walls, the antique chandeliers are festooned with ribbons, and the half-moon windows are rimmed with white lights adding to the ambience. The kitchen is partitioned off with rust-colored blinds, and the familiar sounds that emanate from within add a homey feel to an elegant experience.

The menu changes seasonally, but dinner is strictly fixed price on weekends–four courses with a choice of five or six main dishes—but on weeknights there are also à la carte dinners available.

Chef Peter Morrison is an adventurous young chef whose cuisine reflects the bounty of the season and ingredients fresh from the market stalls that are located below the restaurant. Menu highlights include a Filet of Beef Tenderloin, pan-grilled and served with Cabernet Black Pepper Butter and Carmelized Onions, and Columbia River Sturgeon, roasted in a Cornmeal Crust and served with Apricot-Nectarine Salsa.

Dinner Tuesday–Sunday 5:30PM–10PM
AVERAGE DINNER FOR TWO: $75

Flying Fish Restaurant, Bar and Grill

AMERICAN CUISINE
2234 First Avenue
Seattle, Washington
206-728-8595

The Flying Fish caters to the see-and-be-seen crowd. With its splashy mirrored bar, hand-painted tables, and a two-level dining room that falls somewhere between industrial chic and an island retreat, it has become a favorite. The dining room has floor-to-ceiling glass garage doors and is bathed in soothing Caribbean colors.

This contemporary seafood restaurant prepares local ingredients in ways heretofore not yet seen in Seattle. Flavors are drawn from around the world: the excitement of galanga from Thailand, the intensity of chipotles from Mexico, the brilliance of saffron from Spain.

Menu items include such exotic seafood dishes as Thai Crab Cakes with Lemongrass Mayonnaise, Lobster Tostada with a Black Bean and Corn Salsa, Red Curry Mussel Stew served with a Garlic Crostada and Mango Chutney, and a Roasted Lingcod with Moroccan Chickpea Curry.

Open for Dinner Monday–Saturday 5PM–Midnight
Average Dinner For Two: $50

FULLERS
SHERATON SEATTLE HOTEL AND TOWERS

PACIFIC NORTHWEST CUISINE
1400 Sixth Avenue
Seattle, Washington
206-447-5544

Fullers, located adjacent to the lobby of the Sheraton Seattle Hotel and Towers, offers European ambience created by soft lighting, muted colors, and banquettes. The dining room is highlighted by a custom-designed George Tsutakawa fountain and displays many pieces from the Sheraton Seattle Hotel and Towers' contemporary art collection that is one of the largest permanent public/private collections in the Pacific Northwest. The Pilchuck Glass School has several glass works featured in Fullers.

Chef Monique Andrée Barbeau has won awards and accolades and is constantly mentioned as one of the best chefs in the Pacific Northwest. The cuisine is internationally influenced and regionally inspired.

Naturally, the emphasis is on seafood, but among the signature entrées there is a Moroccan Spiced Quail with Preserved Lemons and Oregano and a Roasted Beet and Greens Salad with Shallot Vinaigrette tossed with Field Greens.

Some of the seafood signature items to try are the Grilled Rare Ahi Tuna with Kimchee Salad and Pickled Vegetables, the house-marinated Kasu Salmon with Gingered Asian Slaw and Eggplant Charmoula, and the Herb-Crusted Sea Scallops with Curried Pesto Broth.

Open for Lunch Monday–Friday 11:30AM–2PM
Dinner Monday–Saturday 5:30PM–10PM
AVERAGE DINNER FOR TWO: $65

Il Bistro

ITALIAN CUISINE
93-A Pike Street
Seattle, Washington
206-682-3049

It's a great room on a dark and stormy night. Underground and intimate, Il Bistro is a candlelit cavern serving Italian food coupled with the best of fresh local products.

What light there is glows soft and warm,, and this spare restaurant has been a midtown favorite for more than a dozen years. Part of that may be due to the dark wood floors, the white linen, and the candlelight on the broad, low archway that leads into the lounge, emanating a sense of subterranean coziness. The atmosphere alone, with its hint of intrigue and hushed conversations, might be worth the visit, but Il Bistro delivers in every way.

The wine list is extensive and complementary to the Tuscan standbys on the menu. The bartenders make magic with a bar that stocks an impressive assortment of chilled vodkas, vintage ports, brandies, cognacs, liqueurs, and over 17 different single malt Scotches.

Chef Dino Daquila's menu contains many unrivaled dishes. Appetizers that are not to be missed are the Antipasto Dino (an assortment of grilled marinated vegetables, meats and cheeses) and the Carpaccio di Vitello (thin slices of veal tenderloin with olive oil, capers, tomato and Parmesan cheese. The Fettuccine with Porcini and Oyster Mushrooms in a Cream Sauce Pasta is a delightful entrée choice that is neither overly complex or heavy. The Rack of Lamb sits in a rich Sangiovese Wine sauce that is so dark and dense it is almost like spooning up wine jam.

Lunch Monday–Friday 11:30AM–2PM
Dinner Sunday–Saturday 5:30PM–10PM
Average Dinner For Two: $100

Il Terrazzo Carmine

ITALIAN CUISINE
411 First Avenue South
Seattle, Washington
206-467-7797

Chef and Owner Carmine Smeraldo opened Il Terrazzo Carmine in 1984 and it has been a favorite since day one.

Il Terrazzo Carmine is an oasis in the middle of downtown Seattle. With a very secluded courtyard offering a fountain, pond, trees, and flowers, the restaurant has a Parisian kind of feeling. The garden flower motif is continued indoors with the flowered drapes and dishes. The decor is Tuscan provincial with lots of wood and tile accents.

The cuisine is regional Italian with an emphasis on the Tuscany area–simple yet delicious. Offering over 13 different pastas, 4 different soups, 13 different meat entrées, and 7 different daily specials, there is something for everyone.

Featured items on the menu are traditional Italian with a modern twist. Appetizers to enjoy are Calamari, pan-sautéed with a little Garlic, Tomato, Parsley and Lemon Juice and an antipasto display of assorted antipastos featuring six different Grilled Eggplants with a splash of Wine Vinegar, Roasted Peppers with Extra-Virgin Olive Oil and Garlic Black Olives, Pickled Mushrooms, Fresh Fish, Calamari Salad and Prosciutto from Parma.

Another favorite is the Cream of Cauliflower Soup, baked and browned with Parmesan Cheese. And do not miss the Tiramisu dessert, a local favorite for over 12 years.

Lunch Monday–Friday 11:30AM–2:30PM
Dinner Monday–Saturday 5:30PM–10:30PM
AVERAGE DINNER FOR TWO: $50

Le Gourmand

PACIFIC NORTHWEST CUISINE
425 Northwest Mark Street
Seattle, Washington
206-784-3463

Le Gourmand is alive with the spirit of a small Parisian restaurant. Often, diners are surprised to hear the waitstaff speaking English. The mood is not stuffy by any means —orders come to the table on large platters and diners help themselves.

Chef-owners Robin Sanders and Bruce Naftaly have created a calm and intimate dining space simply decorated with filmy curtains to obscure traffic, walls of mottled taupe and cream colors and matching carpet, and a mere dozen tables set with fresh linens and carefully arranged seasonal flowers. Robin and Bruce enjoy ferreting out the best local ingredients and using them to the fullest capacity, and then giving credit to the suppliers by listing them on the back of the menu.

The menu is small and prices are fixed. A small party can order the entire menu and everyone can have a taste. Some of the recent highlights included a Glazed Roasted Duck surrounded by a Berry Duck Stock and Cognac Sauce and a Strawberry and Raspberry Tart that includes tiny white strawberries.

Dinner Wednesday–Saturday, 5:30PM–10PM
AVERAGE DINNER FOR TWO: $55

PIROSMANI

MEDITERRANEAN AND GEORGIAN REPUBLIC CUISINE
2220 Queen Anne Avenue North
Seattle, Washington
206-285-3360

One of only three restaurants in the entire country to serve food from the republic of Georgia and the Mediterranean, Pirosmani recently celebrated its third anniversary. Outside, there is a manicured garden and inviting porch for al fresco dining. Go up some steps and inside, plum-colored walls serve as a backdrop for beautiful oils depicting faraway street scenes and broad windows soaking in the last of the day's light.

Chef-owner Laura Dewell fell in love with the Republic of Georgia, and the love affair continues with her cooking. The menu is a blend of the exotic and the usual Mediterranean fare. The menu is divided in half—half Georgian and half Mediterranean.

Her signature dish is a Tuna seasoned with a Syrian Spice Mix and wrapped in Grape Leaves and served with a Walnut, Pomegranate and Roasted Red Pepper Sauce. Other exotic entrees include the Chakapuli and Elarji which is a Lamb Stew with Plums and Tarragon served with a Feta Cheese-infused Polenta and the Khinkali, which is a traditional Georgian appetizer of Pork and Beef Dumplings seasoned with Mint, Onion, Paprika and Green Peppers.

Highlights of the Mediterranean side include a Portuguese Quail appetizer which is marinated with Paprika, Garlic and Brown Ale and Andalusian Scallops that are seared and encrusted with Almonds, Hazelnuts and Garlic.

Dinner Tuesday–Saturday 5:30PM–10PM
AVERAGE DINNER FOR TWO: $65

PONTI SEAFOOD GRILL

PACIFIC NORTHWEST CUISINE
3014 Third North
Seattle, Washington
206-284-3000

In an out-of-the-way neighborhood along the Ship Canal, the Ponti Seafood Grill resembles an airy and open hillside villa with white stucco walls overlooking three central city bridges. Ponti, which means "bridges," is an intimate restaurant using gracious hospitality, the active beauty of an urban canal and lighter, fresher cuisine showing influences from several continents. With a courtyard with terra-cotta tiles, flower pots and a fountain, outdoor dining is a dream-like setting.

The view from every table is 180° through the four bay windows stretching from the bar to the three, intimate dining rooms. The individual dining rooms are expressed in the buildings exterior, which presents a complex massing of shapes, finished in a wood-trimmed stucco and topped with several concrete tiled roof slopes. Every effort is made to incorporate the outdoors by serving on the patio. The restaurant's design has several sensual levels; it complements Ponti's innovative, international cuisine while maximizing the luxurious beauty of its waterfront site.

While the name of the restaurant is Italian, the menu is a culinary hybrid of Asian elements and Pacific Northwest that Chef Alvin Binuya is largely responsible for. His Philippine heritage blends well with the Pacific Rim cuisine. One of the most popular items on the menu is a Brazilian Lobster Stew with Mussels, Tomatoes, Coconut Milk, Ginger and Cilantro Pesto. Other favorites are a Chilean Sea Bass wrapped in Grape Leaves with Pine Nuts, Lemon and Shallots and a Cayenne flour-dredged Monkfish with Ginger-Crayfish Sauce and Eggplant Fritters.

Lunch and Dinner Monday–Saturday 11:30AM–2AM
Sunday 10AM–Midnight
Sunday Brunch 10AM–2:30PM
AVERAGE DINNER FOR TWO: $65

Ray's Boathouse, Café and Catering

PACIFIC NORTHWEST CUISINE
6049 Seaview Avenue Northwest
Seattle, Washington
206-789-3770

Located on Shilshole Bay, Ray's Boathouse, Café and Catering gives the diner an opportunity to enjoy the view of fiery sunsets over the Olympic Mountains.

This is the place to go if you want to learn about seafood—such as different types of mussels—and the wine that goes with it, for the staff is more than happy to teach you. Ray's pursues the freshest of seasonal Pacific Northwest bounty, which allows them to constantly create new dishes as well as continue to offer favorites.

Executive Chef Charles Ramseyer has created an innovative menu for the downstairs Boathouse Restaurant that changes weekly. Entrées worth sampling are an Oregon Coast Albacore Tuna with Ginger-Lime Crumb and Soy Citrus Glaze and the Oregon Coast Troll Red King Salmon basted in a Yakima Valley Peach and Honey Syrup.

The upstairs Café also offers a similar rotation of new dishes in a more casual unstructured atmosphere with an outdoor deck and 20 microbrews on tap. Ray's renowned wine list offers over 400 wines, featuring many crafted in the Pacific Northwest.

Open Dinner: Monday–Friday, 5PM–9:30PM
Saturday & Sunday, 4:30PM–10PM
AVERAGE DINNER FOR TWO: $60

ROVER'S

COUNTRY FRENCH CUISINE
2808 East Madison
Seattle, Washington
206-325-7442

A cozy white cottage done up in country French decor is the setting for the spectacularly acclaimed Rover's. Double doors open onto chef and owner Thierry Rautureau's colorful garden of herbs and edible flowers. The best red, white and sparkling wines rest in a mahogany toned wine chest built into one wall, while sunlight streams into the newly remodeled rooms.

Chef Rautureau has received the highest praise from every reviewer and fellow chef ever to sample his creations. To experience the widest possible range of his creations, order the five course, fixed-price Menu Degustation, also available in a vegetarian version.

Some of his delicious preparations include Beet Soup with Goat Cheese and Sage, Sautéed Sea Scallops and Roasted Chestnut Purée in a Truffle Sauce, Squab and Quail with Braised Cabbage and Wild Mushrooms in Armagnac Sauce, and Chocolate Tart with Kumquat Coulis.

Dinner Tuesday–Saturday 5:30 PM
AVERAGE DINNER FOR TWO: $90

TULIO

ITALIAN CUISINE
1100 Fifth Avenue
Seattle, Washington
206-624-5500

Ideally located near the heart of Seattle's shopping and theater district, Tulio surrounds diners in a charming, cozy, Italian atmosphere. The main entrance is an antique revolving door which leads to an inlaid marble entryway and bar.

In Tulio's main dining area, hand-painted light fixtures suspended from the ceiling are adorned with clusters of grape leaves. The room combines a variety of polished wood tones, varying heights of wainscoting, terra-cotta walls, copper accents, and a collection of art, antique mirrors, and the occasional vintage stringed instrument, set high on a shelf. An old-world plaster molded ceiling extends throughout the restaurant.

Chef Walter Pisano's rustic cuisine reflects the rich roots of the Italian countryside, his affinity for his Italian-American heritage, and the elegance of his classic French training. His unique dishes include Smoked Salmon-filled Ravioli with Asparagus and Lemon Cream Sauce, Black Peppered Pork Loin with Fennel Gratin with Vino Santo Glace, Calzone Quattro Formaggio, and Salmon Roasted in a wood-burning oven with Herbs, Potatoes, and Pancetta Butter.

Open for Breakfast, Lunch and Dinner
Monday–Saturday 7 AM–11 PM
AVERAGE DINNER FOR TWO: $50

Union Bay Café

PACIFIC NORTHWEST CUISINE
3515 Northeast 45th Street
Seattle, Washington
206-527-8364

The Union Bay Café is an intimate oasis of contemporary Northwest cuisine under the tutelage of chef/owner Mark Manley. This intimate, friendly place not only showcases wonderful food and great wine, but also a changing array of art by noted local artists.

Chef Manley takes his inspiration from the season, from his mother's Italian heritage and from the sheer delight in using the very best raw ingredients.

Menu highlights include a Rabbit Pâté with fresh Apricot and Onion Marmalade, Muscovy Duck Breast, roasted with fresh Plums, Garlic, Ginger and Scallions and Loin of Ostrich, grilled with Roasted Sweet Onions and Port Wine Sauce, and topped with Gorgonzola Cheese and Capelli Pasta with Caramelized Squash, Olives, Sun-Dried Tomatoes, Garlic and Tarragon. Bon Appetit!

Open for Dinner Tuesday–Sunday 5PM–10PM
Average Dinner For Two: $50

HOME BY THE SEA

2388 East Sunlight Beach Road
Clinton, Washington 98236
360-321-2964
Room Rates: $145–$165

There are two accommodations at Home By The Sea bed and breakfast. Both are suitable for either couples or single travelers.

The Sunset Room is upstairs in the Main House. It offers a private bath, queen-size bed, gourmet breakfasts and splendid views of Useless Bay and the Olympic Mountains.

The Sandpiper Suite is on the beach and offers a private garden entrance. It includes kitchen, dining and living room areas, wood-burning stove, queen bed, private outdoor Jacuzzi for two and a private deck. The views face west to capture sunsets and it is one step to Useless Bay.

Breakfast baskets filled with homemade baked specialties and local products are delivered to the rooms.

FRENCH ROAD FARM

3841 East French Rd.
Clinton, WA 98236
360-321-2964
Room Rates: $145–$165

The charming 1930s former farmhouse rests on 10 acres of tranquil meadow and woodland. The farmhouse has a bedroom with views of the meadow and a queen-size bed. There is a reading room with shelves full of books—old and new.

The living room has clear fir walls, a Irish enamel pellet stove and French doors which open out to the lawn and gardens. The sun room has picture windows, a slate floor, wicker furniture, plants and gardening books. There is also a farmhouse-style kitchen and an intimate dining room. The completely renovated bath has a 7-foot Jacuzzi bathtub surrounded by tile with a large picture window on one side which looks out onto the private meadow.

A breakfast basket filled with homemade baked specialties and local products is delivered to the French Road Farm.

HUNT CLUB-SORRENTO HOTEL, SEATTLE

900 Madison Street
Seattle, Washington 98104
206-622-6400
800-426-1265
Room Rates: $180–$220

The Sorrento Hotel is a beautiful blend of Italian Renaissance and Seattle character. Understated luxury gives the impression of a fine European residence. The Sorrento Hotel maintains its grand facade designed in 1908 by premier Pacific Northwest architect Harlan Thomas in the tradition of Sorrento, Italy. Terra-cotta trim, mission-style towers and an Italian fountain enhance the canopied carriage entrance. The courteous staff, responds to any request, big or small. Service is a Sorrento specialty of the house.

With 76 guest rooms and suites, the Sorrento Hotel prides itself on the fact that no two rooms are alike. Furnished with antiques, the hotel's old world charm continues throughout the rooms with modern conveniences such as goose-down pillows, bathrobes, oversized bath towels, enhanced sitting and dressing rooms. The luxurious Penthouse Suite showcases a panoramic view of Seattle, outdoor deck with private spa, baby grand piano, and marble wood-burning fireplace.

Chef Eric Lenard creates award-winning cuisine ranging from innovative Northwest to traditional American fare. The intimate Hunt Club is the perfect setting for Lenard's "signature" dishes such as Bourbon-Glazed Northwest Pheasant Breast with Pecan Wild Rice and Watercress, and Alderwood and Rosemary Smoked Rack of Lamb.

The Inn at Swifts Bay

Route 2, Box 3402
Lopez Island, Washington 98261
360-468-3636
Room Rates: $75–$155

Nestled between Swifts and Shoal Bay, the Inn at Swifts Bay enjoys a casual atmosphere that invites guests to kick off their shoes and put their feet up. This Tudor-style inn is comfortable, to say the least. Innkeepers Christopher Brandmeir and Robert Herrmann demand that guests feel pampered and wickedly self-indulgent. Snuggle up on a large chintz-covered sofa and let the fireplace and a sherry warm your body and spirit. Walking along the private beach with Max the Labrador is a peaceful communion with nature, and the stress of the modern world seems an ocean away. Or sign up for private use of the outside hot tub, tucked into the edge of the woods and open to the sky above and let your problems melt away as you immerse yourself in the bubbling waters. The inn will soon be adding a new workout studio that includes a treadmill and sauna.

The casual ambience is carried through to the five bedrooms. Three of the five have private baths. Fresh flowers and books are everywhere you look. All the bedrooms have white goose down or lambswool comforters to dive under when the temperature drops.

Breakfast is served around "9-ish" and is always "sit down" style, never buffet. Each table has a basket of freshly baked muffins, fresh juice, and containers of homemade jam. Entrées may include such selections as Hazelnut Waffles with fresh Lopez Island Berries and Crème Fraîche or Sautéed Apple, Ham and Brie Omelets or Locally Smoked Salmon, Chive and Potato Pancakes. If that was not enough, the fresh muffins are unique creations as well, with past highlights being Pumpkin and Eggnog, Cappuccino, and Fresh Pear.

THE JAMES HOUSE

1238 Washington Street
Port Townsend, Washington 98368
360-385-1238
800-385-1238
Room Rates: $52–$150

The James House, built in 1889, sits on the bluff overlooking the water, mountains of Puget Sound, and historic downtown. The James House is on the National Register of Historic Places as the first bed and breakfast in the Northwest.

Overnights in this fine old mansion are a reminder of another era when the bay was filled with sailing ships and downtown streets were bustling with activity. Now only a short walk away, guests can explore the downtown district filled with fine restaurants, shops, galleries, museums, and the waterfront. Guests taking off in a different direction will find beaches, parks, mansions, historic houses, and beautiful residential gardens.

The James House has only 12 one-of-a-kind rooms and suites available. The Master/Bridal Suite has unsurpassed views of the bay and mountains. With a wood-burning fireplace, sitting room, and private balcony, guests can enjoy the champagne while watching the sunset. The Cascade Garden Suite has two bedrooms, a fireplace, and antique and wicker furnishings. The Olympic View Room is bright, cheery and has westerly views with antique oak furnishings and a queen bed.

A full breakfast is served in the mornings. Guests are offered sherry and freshly baked cookies in the evening while enjoying the wood-burning fireplaces, music, good books, and spectacular views from throughout the house.

THE MANOR FARM INN

26069 Big Valley Road Northeast
Poulsbo, Washington 98370
360-779-4628
Room Rates: $110–$160

The Manor Farm Inn demands that you leave behind the stress of modern life and enter a simpler, slower and softer world. An oasis, located on 25 pastoral acres, welcomes you with French pine antiques, baskets overflowing with flowers, cozy firelit nooks and unpretentious charm. The century-old weathered white farmhouse, its porches and veranda posts framed by delicate rose vines, beckons guests. Inside guests find country French pine antiques rich with patina, baskets overflowing with flowers, cozy firelit nooks and unpretentious charm.

Accommodations are not so much rooms as private retreats. Everywhere you turn there is beauty and serenity to renew your spirit. Guests might see border collies herding sheep or horses, cows and donkeys grazing in the pastures.

The seven rooms are spacious and have their own private baths. The Pig Room, with its many windows overlooking the pasture, is one of the brightest rooms, with wood burning fireplace and private porch. The Sheep Room is very romantic, with its king-sized bed and wood-burning fireplace. The Stable and Tack Rooms each have a comfortable sitting area for two and enclosed garden area overlooking the barn, with king-sized beds.

Guests begin each day with a three-course hot breakfast in the dining room filled with fresh flowers.

THE SALISH LODGE AT SNOQUALMIE FALLS

U.S. Highway 202
P.O. Box 1109
Snoqwualmie, Washington 98065-1109
800-826-6124
Room Rates: $165–$575

In the middle of the Snoqualmie Valley, the Salish Lodge blends into nature as if it belongs. A harmonious blend of rustic and sophisticated, the hotel makes every every effort is made to assure guests absolute comfort. They can enjoy golfing, skiing, hiking, biking, canoeing and fishing. The Salish Lodge Spa pampers guests with massages, exfoliation treatments and two heated therapy pools. The roof-top hot tub is perfect for looking up at the stars and feeling as if there is no one else in the world.

All 91 luxurious rooms are a blend of natural beauty and refined splendor. Every guest room in the lodge has a wood-burning fireplace, oversized whirlpool tub, custom designed furniture and goose down comforters. Each of the rooms has a light and airy feel, due to the clean-lined furniture, pillowed window seats, flagstone fireplaces, and cedar armoire. Modern-day conveniences such as the television, phone, and bathrobes are concealed. Jacuzzis are separated from the bedrooms by a swinging bedroom doors that allows maximum pleasure from the fireplace.

The only thing that could possibly compare with the scenery outside is the cuisine inside. From breakfast to dinner, culinary brilliance is evident. There is a five-course brunch offered. Some of the more interesting entrées are Cider-Steamed Mussels with Applewood Smoke Bacon and Lavender Roasted Lamb. Complementing the food is a wine cellar with one of Washington's most impressive selections of wines and champagnes.

Sun Mountain Lodge

P.O. Box 1000
Winthrop, Washington 98862
509-996-2211
800-572-0493
Room Rates: $54–$270

Sun Mountain Lodge is an incredible 3,000-acre spread that offers 360° views of the North Cascade Mountains and the Methow Valley. Unlike many upscale hotels, this lodge does not try to compete with Mother Nature. Massive timbers, a lava rock fireplace, and an Idaho Quartzite floor bring the outdoors inside.

From the huge wrought iron chandelier in the lobby to the bentwood chairs and handpainted bedspreads in the guest rooms, all the surroundings harmonize with the mountain and its history. The light fixtures, tables, and other furnishings reflect the mining boom of the 1890s. The guest's rooms are luxurious but understated. Rooms in the main lodge have custom-designed quilts on the four-poster beds and vast windows to capture the view.

Imagine taking a swim in the heated outdoor pool as snow reflects the colors of the setting sun. And with over 100 miles of trails, guests can go hiking, mountain biking, horseback riding and of course, skiing. From spring through fall, the roster of activities is seemingly endless. Nature is the focal point at Sun Mountain.

The dining room has floor-to-ceiling windows so that diners can watch the sunset over the Methow Valley while eating such entrées as Four Mushroom Chicken and Barbecued Duck Breast with Brandy Apricot Sauce. Leave room for Mexican Kahlúa Flan dessert.

TURTLEBACK FARM INN

Route 1
Box 650
Eastsound, Washington 98245
360-376-4914
800-376-4914
Room Rates: $70–$160

Built in the late 1800s, the Turtleback Farm Inn, located on Orcas Island, overlooks 80 acres of meadows, pastures, woods and ponds overlooking the lovely Crow Valley. Renovated and expanded in 1985, the inn preserves the original farmhouse while incorporating modern-day conveniences. Guests can enjoy bird watching or leisurely walks all over the grounds.

Each of the seven guest bedrooms have their own bathroom and are furnished with a blend of antiques and contemporary pieces. The views from each of the rooms vary from meadow and orchards to duck ponds and trees. The Meadow View Room has a king bed with antique furnishings and a private deck overlooking the meadow.

It takes a great breakfast feast to lure guests from their enchanting rooms, and this breakfast is it. The inn believes in starting the day off right with a hearty breakfast of farm-fresh eggs and meats, fresh fruits and juices, award-winning granola, home-baked breads and pastries. The strawberry crepes are particularly delicious. All this is served on fine china and linen on a sun-washed deck.

After a day of hiking, fishing, kayaking, sailing, wind surfing or just reading by their pond, return to the Turtleback for a relaxing soak in your private bath or a sherry on the deck overlooking the valley below.

Willcox House

2390 Tekiu Road
Bremerton, Washington 98312
360-830-4492
Room Rates: $115–$175

In 1936, Colonel Willcox selected noted architect Lionel Pries to design a private residence for his family. The result was a 10,000-square foot mansion that was called "the grand entertainment capital of the Canal region."

Located on a shoreline bluff of the Hood Canal, every room of Willcox house is angled to capture glorious vistas of sparkling waters and the Olympic Mountains. In their painstaking restoration of the original grandeur of the house, Cecilia and Philip Hughes have taken care to preserve the integrity of the original design.

The library is one of the grandest rooms, offering views of the Hood Canal and the mountains. The game room is always good for diversions of games of skill or chance. Pool, darts and board games are among the usual favorites. The 300 foot private pier with a floating dock can accommodate guests' boats, or can be used for fishing by guests of Willcox House. There are five marble and copper fireplaces located throughout the inn, offering warmth and companionship for lazy days and quiet nights. Each of the five bedrooms has its own unequaled charms.

Willcox House offers a famous "Country House Inn" breakfast that is served at your private table in the view dining room. Inn guests are invited to make reservations for the prix fixe gourmet dinners.

BADGER MOUNTAIN WINERY

110 Jurupa Street
Kennewick, Washington 99337-1001
509-627-4986
800-643-WINE
Open Daily for Tasting 10AM–5PM
Tours: By Appointment

Since 1988, Badger Mountain has been committed to 100% organic viticulture. No herbicides, insecticides, pesticides, or chemical fertilizers are used, and only approved, naturally occurring substances are applied in the vineyard.

In 1990, Badger Mountain was the first vineyard to be Washington State Certified Organic. It takes two years to gain certification, and state inspectors check records, tissue and soil samples to make sure there is no residue of chemicals. Once certified, the vineyard is subject to unannounced inspections to monitor the organic status.

The vineyard is situated on a south-facing slope in the Columbia Valley. Warm summer sun, deep volcanic soil, and water from mountain snows are essential to the character of the wines. Winemaker Greg Powers oversees the grapes from vine to bottle, creating wines of character and distinction. Recently, Badger Mountain added a new label called "Powers."

Bainbridge Island Vineyards and Winery

682 State Highway 305
Bainbridge Island, Washington 98110
206-842-9463
Open noon to 5PM Wednesdays–Sundays. Tours at 2PM Sundays

Bainbridge Island Vineyards and Winery grow vinefera grapes on the island that is within sight of downtown Seattle. With only 6 ½ acres, they are Seattle's only local winery.

Growing a variety of grapes from France and Germany that are not commonly available in the supermarkets and liquor stores, they delight in being a little different from the rest.

On display in the tasting room is a collection of antique and unique drinking vessels. The bulk of the collection centers around wine glasses from the 1600s to the 1900s. The Bentryn family plants, trains, prunes, and weeds their own vines, giving them a sense of reality and pride in the wines.

Producing only 2000 cases per year, the winery sells out all the wines before the next vintage can replace them. All of Bainbridge wines are sold only at the winery or in a few selected restaurants.

BONAIR WINERY

500 South Bonair Road
Zillah, Washington 98953
509-829-6027
800-882-8939
Open Daily from 10AM–5PM

Bonair Winery is the culmination of Gail and Shirley Puryear's dream, which began when they moved to California in 1968 as newlyweds and often visited the Napa Valley. A hobby of amateur winemaking began, becoming a serious vocation as the years passed.

In 1979, they had the opportunity to return to their native Yakima Valley. Aware of the potential growth of the Yakima Valley wine industry, they decided the time was right to start making their dream a reality, in the summer of 1985, the Puryears decided the time was right to start their own winery. In six hectic weeks the winery was built and equipped. Final approval from the Bureau of Alcohol, Tobacco, and Firearms was received one day before the first crush, and Bonair Winery was born with a first-year production of 1500 gallons.

The 1993 crush was about 14,000 gallons, and production will only expand with sales. The vineyards and winery are a family operation and offer a pleasant contrast to larger, less personal operations.

CHATEAU STE. MICHELLE VINEYARDS AND WINERY

One Stimson Lane
Woodinville, Washington 98072
206-488-1133
Open Daily 10AM–4:30PM
Route: From Interstate 405 north or southbound, take the Winatchee-Monroe Exit #23 East. This will put you on Highway 522 eastbound. Take the first exit (Woodinville Exit) and at the top of the off ramp stay to your right. Go to the second stoplight and again turn right onto 175th. Go to stop sign and turn left. You will now be on Highway 202 East-bound. Stay on the road for approximately two miles, and Chateau Ste. Michelle will be on your right just after the bend in the road.

Founded in 1934, Chateau Ste. Michelle is located on lush and immaculate Washington land. Originally, it was dedicated to fruit wines but in the 1960s, Chateau Ste. Michelle began producing vinifera varietals. The corporate headquarters are housed in an antique-filled mansion once owned by a Seattle lumber baron on the Woodinville property. The mansion and grounds invite guests to enjoy the pathways and trout ponds.

There are over eleven different types of grapes planted on the land producing over 15 different types of wines including Grenache Rosé, Fumé Blanc and Muscat Canelli. They also grow loganberries to produce a Loganberry liqueur.

Over the years, while winning scores of awards, Chateau Ste. Michelle has become one of Washington's largest wineries.

CHINOOK WINES

Route: Immediately East of Exit 82, Off I-82, at the Corner of Wittkopf and Wine Country Raods
P.O. Box 387
Prosser, Washington 99350
509-786-2725
Open for Tastings Friday–Sunday 12PM–5PM

ay Simon and Clay Mackey combined their extensive experience in winemaking and viticulture to begin Chinook Wines in 1983. Since then, Chinook has become synonymous with a limited amount of highly acclaimed dry wines.

Clay and Kay enjoy making wines intended to complement Northwest cuisine. They married and released their first wine in August of 1984.

The original farm buildings house the winery, barrel storage and tasting room. A shaded lawn serves as a picnic area. Bounded by a new vineyard and plum and cherry orchards, the winery is a favorite stop on the newly emergent Yakima Valley tasting trail.

Hoodsport Winery, Inc.

N. 23501 Highway 101
Hoodsport, Washington 98548
360-877-9894
Open Daily 10AM–6PM

Founded in 1980, Hoodsport Winery is an award-winning winery framed against the snow-capped Olympic Mountains and the Hood Canal.

Hoodsport has managed to create, along with the favorites such as Raspberry Wine, more unconventional wines such as Rhubarb Wine, Loganberry Wine and Gooseberry Wine.

While Hoodsport is famous for its fruit wines, it also produces an award-winning Island Belle wine made from a native American grape descendant.

Guests can sample the different types of grape varieties and Hoodsport's famous Raspberry Wine Chocolate Truffle.

Kiona Vineyards and Winery

Route 2, Box 2169E
Benton City, Washington 99320
509-588-6716
Open Daily for Tasting: Noon–5PM

Kiona Vineyards was founded by the Williams and Holmes families in 1972 with the purchase of 86 acres of raw land in south eastern Washington. Literally translated, in the Yakima Indian language Kiona means "brown hills." No fences, structures, or roads marred the landscape.

The partners recognized the site as one that would combine the bright, fruity variety intensity from the cooler upper Yakima Valley with the rich, full-bodied character expected from the warmer Columbia basin just two miles away. Combined with these ideal climatic conditions is a deep, well-drained, chalk like soil structure, which is in some ways similar to that of the finest vineyards in Europe.

Before the dream could begin, irrigation wells were drilled through 500 feet of solid rock, electricity was brought in from three miles away, and new roads were platted. The first acreage was planted in 1975 and expanded in later years to 30 acres.

In 1994, Jim Holmes retired as a partner, and Kiona is now solely owned by the Williams family. The initial Kiona crush in 1980 was 1,200 gallons; in 1993 over 36,000 were made. Recent growth has been concentrated on producing world-class red wines.

Orcas Wine Company

Orcas Island
Porter Station Building
Horseshoe Highway
P.O. Box 34
Eastsound, Washington 98245
360-376-6244
800-934-7616
Open Daily for Tasting 11AM–6PM

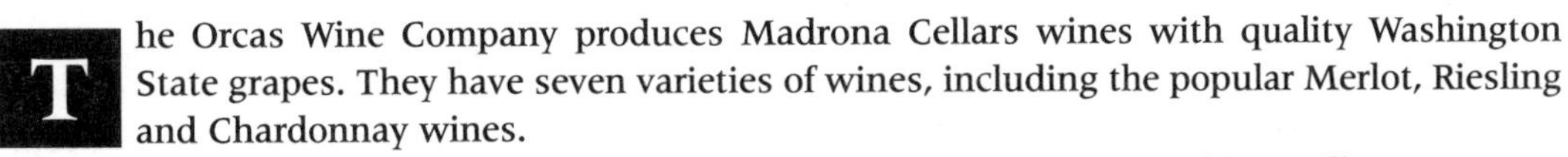

The Orcas Wine Company produces Madrona Cellars wines with quality Washington State grapes. They have seven varieties of wines, including the popular Merlot, Riesling and Chardonnay wines.

Peeking through bright red and yellow flowers, guests can enjoy watching sailboats maneuvering on the bay from the wine shop. The Orcas Wine Company has recently opened an oyster wine bar adjacent to their wine shop on Eastsound's waterfront with a spectacular view of the Sound.

Pontin Del Roza

35502 North Hinzerling Road
Prosser, Washington 99350
509-786-4449
Open Daily 10AM–5PM

Beginning several centuries ago in the northwest part of Italy, a wine-growing tradition was established by the Pontin family. A pioneering spirit brought some of the Pontin family to the Yakima Valley over 60 years ago. Pontin Del Roza translates roughly from Italian to mean, "Pontin family farm on the Roza."

The winery founded by Scott Pontin uses the grapes grown only from "the Roza," an area of south-facing slopes along the north side of the Yakima Valley. The Pontin family have been farming for over 30 years. They chose a site and planted the first wine grapes... from the old world to the new world, traditional and modern methods for the classic European wine flavor.

Over the years, Pontin Del Roza has carefully selected the grape varieties to fit the climate and soil. The Pontin family plans a gradual growth within the industry, while remaining a small family-owned winery producing only the finest premium quality wines.

TEFFT CELLARS

1320 Independence Road
Outlook, Washington 98938
509-837-7651
Open Friday–Monday 12PM–5PM
Route: Take I-82 to Exit 63 and follow the blue tourist signs

Owners Joel and Pam Tefft's experience with wine began over 10 years ago with an introduction to premium wines. Thus began a slow progression into the total enjoyment of fine wine. As they learned more about wine, the more intrigued they became with the winemaking process. This great interest in winemaking brought them to Washington State on vacation to tour the wine country. They decided to move to the Yakima Valley in 1987 and purchased an existing Concord vineyard with the hope of eventually replanting vinifera and making wine. Armed with nothing more than a great interest in wine, they began the process of establishing a winery. Tefft Cellars became a reality on November 4, 1991 when they were officially licensed as a winery. The dream had come true.

WASHINGTON HILLS CELLARS

111 East Lincoln Avenue
Sunnyside, Washington 98033
509-839-9463
Open Daily for Tasting 11AM–5:30PM
Tours: By Appointment

The story of Washington Hills Cellars begins in the late 1980s, when one of the state's most knowledgeable wine retailers and distributors and one of the Northwest's best winemakers combined their talents and experience in a new business venture.

Harry D. Alhadeff, who had owned the La Cantina chain of wine shops and restaurants and Brian Carter, a winemaker of extraordinary depth and experience, decided that creating a new winery together would allow each of them to do what he loved best—for Brian, making the best wines possible, for Harry, marketing them to an increasingly wine-savvy public—while bringing to the consuming public consistently excellent wines. And they could have fun doing it.

Washington Hills Cellars was launched in 1988 with 50,000 gallons of wine—the first vintage Brian Carter ever made for the new winery and a new brand—Washington Hills Cellars.

By 1991, Washington Hills had acquired the facility and launched an ongoing program of modernization and improvement that included installing state-of-the-art equipment, and adding a tasting room, retail store and gardens for picnics and special events.

Today, Washington Hills Cellars is one of Washington's largest and most respected wineries. Its three brands, Washington Hills, W.B. Bridgman and Apex, cover the spectrum of wines from premium to super ultrapremium. All three of the winery's brands have received glowing reviews from the most respected wine experts here and abroad.

YAKIMA RIVER WINERY

143302 North River Road
Prosser, Washington 99350
509-786-2805
Open Dialy for Tasting 10AM–5PM

In 1977, John and Louise Rauner founded the Yakima River Winery in the heart of the Yakima Valley, Washington State's premier wine area. In the first year, they produced 1000 cases of virtually handmade wine.

The family that owns the winery makes the wine, and they are professionals who care greatly about their work and believe quality cannot be compromised. Yakima River has grown by incorporating advanced technology and automation in a carefully considered program that ensures the quality will not be sacrificed to production.

From the beginning to the present, the winery has produced wines which consistently have been awarded honors in competition and in consumer preference. From label and foil design to point-of-sale material, Yakima River Winery says "premium wine" to consumers.

British Columbia

THE ALABASTER RESTAURANT

NORTHERN ITALIAN CUISINE
1168 Hamilton Street
Vancouver, British Columbia, Canada
604-687-1758

Taking its name from the alabaster sculpture of Venus in the center of the room, the Alabaster Restaurant is a favorite with locals and well-informed visitors alike.

With its brick walls and crystal chandeliers, the Alabaster is an eclectic place where food is the focus. There are no presentation gimmicks, exotic ingredients or cross-culturalism; just terrific Northern Italian cuisine.

Chef/owner Markus Wieland is serious about his craft and prefers to perfect it in subtler ways. The menu changes seasonally but favorites are kept. Every entrée is well thought out and a flawless balance of flavors, colors and textures.

The Alabaster's signature dishes include a spicy Tuscan-style fish broth with sauté of seasonal fish and shellfish and a veal saltimbocca served with a mushroom risotto. Other highlights include Grilled Veal Steak with Pan-fried Polenta, Sautéed Tiger Prawns with a Champagne, Grapefruit and Tarragon Butter Sauce, and Linguine with Peperoncini-Marinated Grilled Lamb Loin, Roasted Peppers, Garlic, Oregano and Extra-Virgin Olive Oil.

With a very dignified, calm air, The Alabaster is comfortably arranged, offering attentive service where no customer is left waiting.

Lunch Monday–Friday, 11:30AM–2PM
Dinner Monday–Saturday, 5:30PM–1AM
AVERAGE DINNER FOR TWO: $90

Caffe de Medici Restaurant

NORTHERN ITALIAN CUISINE
109-1025 Robson Street
Vancouver, British Columbia, Canada
604-669-9322

Tucked away from the bustle of the street, the wonderfully romantic Caffe de Medici Restaurant specializes in Northern Italian cuisine. With a backdrop of antique carpets, high arched ceilings, muraled walls, elaborate chandeliers and portraits of the Medici family, this polished restaurant remains a favorite for locals and visitors alike.

Artistically decorated in forest green and maroon, the restaurant's rich ambiance is carried through to the food. Executive Chef Gino Punzo creates amazing dishes such as Veal and Prawn Rolls. Abundant with fresh seafood, the cuisine specialties also include chicken breasts stuffed with prawns, spinach draped in a papaya salsa and a white chocolate mousse that is sinful to look at—much less eat.

Other must-tries include an antipasto assortment of shrimps, scallops, eggplant, mussels, clams, prosciutto, and home-cured olives that is large enough to share, as well as the fettuccine della casa filled with prosciutto, chicken and peas in a cream sauce. Delicious!

Open Lunch Monday–Friday, 11:30AM–2:30PM
Open Dinner Monday–Sunday, 5PM–10:30PM
AVERAGE DINNER FOR TWO: $100

Heron's Restaurant & Lounge

PACIFIC NORTHWEST CUISINE
900 Canada Place Way
Vancouver, British Columbia, Canada
604-691-1991

Heron's Restaurant and Lounge features two stories of floor-to-ceiling windows allowing a panoramic view of the snowcapped north shore mountains and cruise ships gliding into Vancouver's shores. When weather permits, diners can enjoy their meal on the patio closer to the water's edge.

Executive Chef Daryle Ryo Nagata believes food must be consistently fresh, creative in presentation and extraordinary in taste, with no exceptions. Born of a Scottish mother and Japanese father, he enjoys combining regional ingredients and various cultures into what he calls "fusion food."

Heron's cuisine rivals the scenery with an à la carte menu, breakfast and lunch buffets and a dinner menu with 16 salmon specialties. Daryle is noted for his salmon creations, featuring smoked salmon, pan-seared salmon with spinach and ginger, and marinated salmon with maple and bourbon sauce.

Open Daily 6:30AM–10PM
Sunday Brunch 11:30AM–3PM
AVERAGE DINNER FOR TWO: $65

La Rúa Restaurante

MEDITERRANEAN CUISINE
4557 Blackcomb Way
Whistler, British Columbia, Canada
604-932-5011

alking into La Rúa, diners enter a restaurant where fine dining is an adventure. When Chef Mario Enero opened La Rúa Restaurante to give his imagination freedom to explore the outer limits of food preparation, his fans followed him.

The cuisine is ahead of the rest of the pack of high-end eateries. Some specialties of the house include Baked Sea Bass with Crazy Herbs in a Red Wine Sauce, Filet Mignon of Veal with Roasted Artichokes and Mushrooms and Mussels steamed with a Cilantro Tomato Concasse and Figs.

Pasta specials feature a Butternut Squash Agnolotti in a curry cream sauce with Smoked Duck, and Taglierini Spinach Pesto with Pepper, Tomato and Zucchini Chutney.

All desserts are homemade on the premises.

Open Dinner: Sunday–Thursday, 5:30PM–10PM
Friday–Saturday, 5:30PM–11PM
AVERAGE DINNER FOR TWO: $80

Le Crocodile

FRENCH CUISINE
100-909 Burrard Street
Vancouver, British Columbia, Canada
604-669-4298

It is no secret that Le Crocodile is one of Vancouver's finest restaurants. Chef/Owner Michel Jacob is always on hand to make every guest feel welcome. Since it's a favorite with the "in" crowd, diners can spot celebrities enjoying the uncomplicatedbut sophisticated fare.

Decorated in Van Gogh-mustard yellow and mahogany, this is the place to go for a special occasion. It is humming with the happy congeniality, spontaneous laughter and spirited energy that is typical of a French bistro.

The setting is enhanced by a staff that is so hospitable that even solo diners do not feel alone. Time and time again, it has been voted the best French restaurant in the city.

Michel practices the cuisine of his native Alsace with no patience for anything short of perfection. His motto is that if you want to be a good chef you must know the basics.

For over 10 years, the savory, warm Alsatian Onion Tart starter and the Tomato Gin soup have been signatures of Le Crocodile. Other menu highlights include Grilled Atlantic Scallops with Basil Butter Sauce served with Black Squid Ink Linguine, Fresh Roasted Leg of Lamb served with Onion Confit and Minted Jus, and for dessert, a wonderful Whole Poached Pear with Chocolate Mousse and Raspberry Coulis.

Lunch Monday–Friday 11:30AM–2:30PM
Dinner Monday–Saturday 5:30PM–10:30PM
AVERAGE DINNER FOR TWO: $60

Le Club-The Sutton Place Hotel

CONTINENTAL CUISINE
845 Burrard Street
Vancouver, British Columbia, Canada
604-682-5511

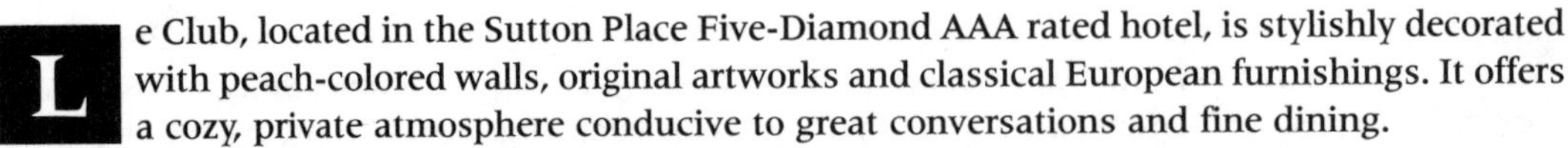

Le Club, located in the Sutton Place Five-Diamond AAA rated hotel, is stylishly decorated with peach-colored walls, original artworks and classical European furnishings. It offers a cozy, private atmosphere conducive to great conversations and fine dining.

The restaurant, under the direction of Chef Kai Lermen, features daily specialties of the very best in light and modern cuisine inspired by the cooking of continental Europe.

Among the entrées served are market specialties of the day, featuring innovative sauces, and creative fish dishes. Rave reviews from gourmets worldwide praise Chef Lermen's Veal Loin with Foie Gras in a Calvados Sauce, Grilled Ahi Tuna on Jalapeño Linguine with a Papaya Tomato Salsa, and Breast of Pheasant with Pineapple Champagne Cabbage in a Balsamic Vinegar Sauce.

Open Dinner: Monday–Saturday 5PM–10PM
AVERAGE DINNER FOR TWO: $80

Monterey Lounge & Grill Pacific Palisades Hotel

PACIFIC NORTHWEST CUISINE
1277 Robson Street
Vancouver, British Columbia, Canada
604-688-0461

Monterey Lounge & Grill at the Pacific Palisades Hotel has opened its much-loved patio in the heart of downtown Vancouver. Locals and visitors alike share the tradition of sun-shaded breakfasts and lunches or sunset diners on the patio. With friendly service complemented by a relaxed atmosphere, the innovative West Coast menu is a standout from the usual restaurant fare.

Fresh ingredients are prepared with enthusiasm to come together in a variety of pastas, seafoods, salads, desserts and local wines. Dinner is a celebration of salmon–strips of white spring salmon marinated in rock salt, brown sugar, maple syrup, then cold-smoked and hot-smoked for 14 hours, or a silken salmon mousse with dark rye wafers.

Not to disappoint meat lovers, the broiled sirloin is married with a homemade peppermint mustard. Desserts are more uniquely Canadian, offering baby pumpkins filled with pumpkin cheesecake and organic Okanagan apples tossed with fresh rosemary and baked in cinnamon pastry.

Open Daily for Breakfast, 6:30AM
Open Daily for Lunch, 11:30AM–2:30PM
Open Daily for Dinner, 5PM–10PM
AVERAGE DINNER FOR TWO: $85

Raintree Restaurant at the Landing

PACIFIC NORTHWEST CUISINE
375 Water Street
Gastown, Vancouver, British Columbia, Canada
604-688-5570

The Raintree Restaurant celebrates Pacific Northwest cuisine, offering a testimonial of the best that the region has to offer.

Chef Herb Quinn has developed signature dishes focusing on the hearty, with healthy and robust delicacies such as Queen Charlotte Island's Dungeness Crab, Organic Ranch Beef, Pender Harbour Spot Prawns, Wild Pacific Salmon, and Spring Lamb.

The West Coast theme is continued throughout the wine cellar, boasting award-winning wines from British Columbia, Washington, Oregon, Idaho and California.

Lunch Monday–Friday
Daily for Dinner from 5:30PM
Weekend Brunch
AVERAGE DINNER FOR TWO: $80

SEASONS IN THE PARK RESTAURANT

PACIFIC NORTHWEST CUISINE
Queen Elizabeth Park, Cambie at 33rd
Vancouver, British Columbia, Canada
604-874-8008

At the Seasons in the Park Restaurant, immense windows and skylights overlook the treetops and high-rise buildings of Vancouver, offering the illusion of dining outdoors. The white linen table cloths with burgundy napkins are accented by the wood chairs and the lush green foliage of the plants.

Chef Pierre Delcôte has extensive experience in kitchens throughout Europe and the South Pacific, which he brings to the Seasons. The cuisine is a mixture of the usual favorites and the exotic.

The menu contains tried-and-true entrées such as the Roast Rack of Lamb with a Martini & Rossi Jus and the Grilled Filet Mignon with Brandy and Peppercorn Sauce, as well as the unique Lemon Pepper Linguini with Candy Coho Salmon and Roasted Red Peppers and a Baked Herb-Crusted Chilean Sea Bass that melts in your mouth.

For starters, try the Stuffed Mushrooms with Crab and Shrimp or the Dungeness Crab Ravioli appetizer.

Open Daily for Lunch, 11:30AM–2:30PM
Open Daily for Dinner, 5:30PM–9PM
AVERAGE DINNER FOR TWO: $70

Star Anise Restaurant

FRANCO-AMERICAN CUISINE
1485 West 12th Avenue
Vancouver, British Columbia, Canada
604-737-1485

The Star Anise Restaurant, one of the leading restaurants in Vancouver, is a unique blend of basic Franco-American fare with touches of Italian and Asian cuisines. It's a distinct combination of food that diners might not otherwise have a chance to sample.

Opened in 1993, owner Sammy Lalji is the maitre d'. His graciousness makes you feel like the most important customer ever to walk in the door of his restaurant.

The huge bouquets of flowers are echoed in the big paintings that cover the mustard-yellow walls. The tables are covered with discreet white linen that offsets the wood furniture and dark carpeting.

Chef Julian Bond has created some of the most incredible entrées. The Warm Sausage of Crab and Shrimp set on a spicy Coleslaw is a combination of pure, sweet seafood held together by a micro-thin casing. Other Star Anise specialties are the Five-Spice Marinated Sea Bass, pan-seared on a bed of Saffron and Thyme Gnocchi, oven-roasted Ostrich layered on a bed of Scrambled Eggs in a nest of Vegetables, and Grilled Enokis in a Tomato Risotto with Shiitake and Button Mushrooms.

The wine selection rivals any big restaurant and is changed on a weekly basis.

Open Daily for Dinner, 5:30PM–10PM
AVERAGE DINNER FOR TWO: $90

TOJO'S RESTAURANT

JAPANESE CUISINE
202-777 West Broadway
Vancouver, British Columbia, Canada
604-872-8050

Sushi Chef Hidekazu Tojo is a master at keeping his steady stream of loyal customers happy and entertained. Most of his clientele want to sit ringside at the10-seat sushi bar that is the centerpiece of the restaurant where Tojo is endlessly innovative, surgically precise, and committed to fresh ingredients. But diners who do not get a cherished ringside seat cannot be disappointed because the dining room has a stunning view of the North Shore mountains.

The menu is seasonal since Tojo insists on the freshest ingredients. In the fall, try the pine mushroom soup or the cherry blossoms with scallops and deep fried sole with tiger prawns.

Tojo's talent is in transforming familiar delicacies into the new, making the sushi, sashimi, temaki, nigiri, robata, tempura, and teppan yaki sublime.

Tojo's has three simple rules: Tastes good...looks good...good for you.

Open Daily for Dinner
AVERAGE DINNER FOR TWO: $75

VAL D'ISÈRE

FRENCH CUISINE
4433 Sundial Place, Village Center
Whistler, British Columbia, Canada
604-932-4666

After a long day of skiing down the slopes, you'll find Val d'Isère Restaurant is a treasure. Located in the heart of Whistler Village, Chef/Owner Roland Pfaff welcomes you to the pleasures of the dining table.

Diners are invited to come and enjoy a relaxing evening with wonderful food, great wines and decadent desserts. Val d'Isère is the first-class restaurant where savvy skiers come to reload on consistently good food.

Roland has created several entrées that express his innovative approach to cooking with healthy and seasonal ingredients that are readily available and rarely extravagant.

Among the favorites are the House Onion Pie, the Ostrich Steak with Sun-dried Blueberry Jus and Iced Lemon Soufflé.

Open Daily for Dinner
AVERAGE DINNER FOR TWO: $90

APRIL POINT LODGE

900 April Point Road
Campbell River, British Columbia,
Canada V9W 4Z9
604-285-2222
Room Rates: $99–$395

The April Point Lodge, a favorite of the adventurous traveler for 50 years, offers spectacular coastal scenery, fine salmon fishing, excellent dining, and the hospitality of the Peterson family. Guests enjoy getting close to nature while hiking, cycling or horseback riding on the Island's winding trails.

Accommodations vary, offering rooms with harbor views or six-bedroom guest houses with private hot tubs and Jacuzzi baths.

Chef Dory Ford has created a menu that is hearty, yet elegant fare. A well-stocked wine cellar complements the selections of fresh seafood as well as the finest cuts of beef, lamb and veal.

A unique feature at the April Point Lodge is the twice-weekly barbecues where Eric Peterson, the owner, puts his culinary expertise on display.

THE BEACONSFIELD INN

998 Humboldt Street
Victoria, British Columbia,
Canada V8V 2Z8
604-384-4044
Room Rates: $105–$350

Con and Judi Sollid, Beaconsfield's owners and creative spirits, believe that guests should feel pampered. Built in 1905, the Beaconsfield Inn is an Edwardian hideaway from the modern world. The ambiance makes guests feel as if they have stepped into another era.

With only nine rooms, and suites filled with exquisite antiques, the inn feels more like a private home of a English lord than a hotel.

A delightful full breakfast is served in the restored dining room or in the sunroom, and fireside refreshments of tea, sherry and hors d'oeuvres are served in the library daily. The menu is delicious, using flowers and herbs grown in the garden.

Copper Beech House

1590 Delkatlah
New Masset, Haida Gwaii
Queen Charlotte Islands, Canada V0T 1M0
604-626-5441
Room Rates: $100–$225

At the Copper Beech House, located on the historically rich Queen Charlotte Islands, David Phillips has managed to create a world-class bed and breakfast.

Built in 1914, Copper Beech House started as a seaside saltbox in Naden Harbour, 50 sea miles to the west, and was moved to Watun River on Masset Inlet when the cannery relocated in 1921. It was pulled to its present location by oxen and a stump puller.

In 1980, David acquired the historic property and proceeded to host many government ministers, heads of state and commissions. Copper Beech is constantly being renovated to make it the most comfortable experience possible for its guests, so that anyone feels like a head of state.

DURLACHER HOF

Box 1125
7055 Nesters Road
Whistler, British Columbia,
Canada V0N 1B0
604-932-1924
Room Rates: $110–$195

Hosts Erika and Peter Durlacher wanted to create a traditional Austrian inn where the guests feel pampered and well cared-for. The staff places fresh bouquets of flowers on the dresser of each guest room. A basket of slippers is left by the front door, so the moment guests arrive, they can slip them on and feel right at home.

White stucco walls are a wonderful backdrop to a natural wood balcony that in the summertime is a picture perfect frame for the brilliant flowers that abound.

Famous for its skiing, Durlacher Hof is located only a short walk from the lifts. If snuggling up with your loved one sounds better to you, this bed and breakfast was voted one of the best places to kiss.

In the kitchen, Erica creates a menu that is a mixture of old European recipes with a lighter touch, which suits the decor and atmosphere. Taking advantage of fresh seasonal local ingredients, Erica has several recipes that keep the guests raving long after their departure.

HASTINGS HOUSE

160 Upper Ganges Road
Salt Spring Island
British Columbia,
Canada V8K 2S2
604-537-2362
800-661-9255
Room Rates: $275–$325

Pamper yourself with a visit to the Hastings House. This thirty-acre seaside estate is located on one of the beautiful Gulf Islands that is accessible by boat or plane.

Each suite has its own special atmosphere and charm. Located in five different restored buildings, the staff adds ambiance with personal touches including down comforters, oversized bath towels, and stacks of split firewood for the private fireplace. The Post Suite is a garden cottage, set under a large pear tree, featuring French doors that open onto a beautifully manicured lawn and an ocean view.

Meals are special fare at Hastings House. A full breakfast is delivered to the guests' suites every morning, and afternoon tea is served in the Manor House.

Holland House Inn

595 Michigan Street
Victoria, British Columbia,
Canada V8V 1S7
604-384-6644
800-335-6117
Room Rates: $69–$173

With only ten guest rooms, the Holland House Inn considers itself the perfect small hotel. Located two blocks from Victoria's Inner Harbour, guests can walk to Beacon Hill Park, the Parliament buildings, the British Columbia Provincial Museum, and downtown shopping. This small inn is filled with works of fine art that help create an atmosphere of casual elegance.

You can relax by the fireplace or browse in the art library located in the Gallery Lounge. Collections of original paintings, drawings and sculptures are changed periodically, attesting to the rich artistic community of Victoria.

Rooms are individually designed and feature original works by the premier artists of the city. Bright and lovely, all the rooms have private bathrooms, and some have fireplaces. Queen-sized beds with goose down duvets, antique furnishings and small balconies make each of the rooms a private haven.

HOTEL VANCOUVER

900 West Georgia Street
Vancouver, British Columbia,
Canada V6C 2W6
604-684-3131
800-441-1414
Room Rates: $160–$2,580

With a distinctive green copper roof, exterior carvings, modern conference facilities and elegant guest rooms, the Hotel Vancouver is Vancouver's landmark hotel. Built in 1939, it is now a heritage building that manages to blend the gracious elegance of the past with modern conveniences.

With over 500 guest rooms, the Hotel Vancouver can accommodate even the most demanding traveler. All guest rooms have been refurbished, and traditional touches like hand stenciling and wall moldings give an old-world feeling.

Located in the heart of the city, guests can enjoy many of Vancouver's attractions including the Ford Centre for the Performing Arts, Library Square, General Motors Place sports stadium, the Vancouver Art Gallery and Aquarium. The city's mild climate permits guests to partake in the endless variety of recreational activities accessible from the hotel.

Oceanwood Country Inn

630 Dinner Bay Road
Mayne Island, British Columbia,
Canada V0N 2J0
604-539-5074
Room Rates: $120–$295

Oceanwood Country Inn is situated on 10 private acres of forested land overlooking the Navy Channel of the Gulf Islands. A ferry ride away from Vancouver or Victoria, it is a perfect refuge from the pressures of city life. Marilyn and Jonathan Chilvers are the owners and innkeepers who say that at the Oceanwood Country Inn guests can do whatever they please. If that is enjoying a breakfast of Orange French Toast with fresh raspberry purée and homemade sausage or sitting in a hot tub counting the stars, go ahead. Enjoy. Relax.

Remodeled in 1990 and rebuilt in 1995, each of the 12 guest bedrooms has its own name to match its unique personality. The Wisteria Suite has a soaking tub on one of the two private decks, sunken living room with fireplace, and spacious bathroom with small deck and powder room.

The dining room has a wall of glass doors that open for dining al fresco, and in the evening, guests can watch the sunset reflected off nearby Pender Island. The cuisine emphasizes fresh seasonal items from Oceanwood's own garden and local suppliers. The wine cellar features west coast wines from British Columbia to California.

THE OLD FARMHOUSE

1077 North End Road
Salt Spring Island, British Columbia,
Canada V8K 1L9
604-537-4113
Room Rates: $125–$150

As the name implies, Gerti and Karl Fuss operate this delightful bed and breakfast from their gray and white saltbox farmhouse set in a quiet meadow.

Built in 1895, the main house is a registered historic property. Centrally located, guests can enjoy St. Mary Lake, golf, tennis, Ganges village, and all ferry terminals to get to the mainland.

Sunlight filters through lace curtains in the guest rooms, accenting the pine bedsteads, down comforters, floral chintz fabrics and wicker chairs. Each of the four double rooms has its own private bath. The two upstairs bedrooms have cathedral ceilings and private balconies.

A homemade breakfast is served daily in the dining room.

Sooke Harbour House

1528 Whiffen Spit Road
Sooke, British Columbia,
Canada V0S 1N0
604-642-3421
Room Rates: $108–$235

Sooke Harbour House is perched on a bluff overlooking the Sooke Inlet, offering sweeping views of the Strait of Juan de Fuca and Washington's Olympic Mountains.

Innkeepers Fredrica and Sinclair Philip have created a wonderfully romantic little white inn by the sea, surrounded by over 400 varieties of herbs, flowers, berries and fruit trees. The staff is more than happy to organize fishing charters, nature walks, scuba diving trips and kayaking lessons for guests.

Every room is filled with antique furniture, handsewn quilts and many original artworks. All the guest rooms have an ocean view, balcony or terrace, private bath and fireplace.

Thanks to Sinclair, the cuisine is Northwest fare at its best. Seafood dominates, with purple-hinged rock scallops, sea cucumber, wild mussels, salmon, pink-singing scallops, wolf eel, purple and green sea urchins, shrimp, and king and rock crab that Sinclair gathers while scuba diving. Under the spell of Sooke's masterful chefs, the land and sea gardens blend to create award-winning cuisine of the Pacific Northwest.

THE WEDGEWOOD HOTEL

845 Hornby Street
Vancouver, British Columbia,
Canada V6Z 1V1
604-689-7777
800-663-0666
Room Rates: $110–$300

Located in the heart of Vancouver, this 93-room hotel is the dream child of two sisters, Eleni Skalbania and Joanna Tsaparas. Receiving special permission from Lord Wedgwood (a frequent guest), the sisters chose the name to denote the quality, but added an extra "e." The staff keeps guest histories so that special needs are taken care of even before they are spoken.

Quality is shown in the wallpaper and the carpets from England and in the English antiques that were hand-picked by the sisters. Marble, brass and polished woods welcome upscale clientele. Each of the rooms and suites is enhanced by original artwork and its own flower box-filled balcony.

The Bacchus Ristorante and Chef Alan Groom create a menu of fresh and simple Northern Italian cuisine that is delicious, yet keeps in mind contemporary concerns for healthier, lighter fare. Most nights there are live jazz and blues bands that entice the diner to work off the calories with a romantic turn around the floor.

Calona Vineyards

1125 Richter Street
Kelowna, British Columbia
Canada V1Y 2K6
604-762-9144
Wine Shop Open Daily 10AM–5PM
Tours: 11AM–3PM Daily

Founded in 1932, the Calona Winery is dedicated to excellence in its wines. Winemaster Howard Soon is a 15 year veteran to the wine industry and continues to push the limits of quality to produce award-winning wines. "The race for quality has no finish line," reflects the direction Calona Vineyards strives to achieve with it premium VQA line of wines. Quality grapes, skilled winemaking and superior equipment come together to produce prize-winning wines.

From Trilogy to the Artist Series to the exclusive Private Reserve line, there will be no compromise on quality.

In the cozy cellar-like tasting room, you will be able to experience the marriage of the wines and palatable food selections.

GRAY MONK ESTATE WINERY AND VINEYARDS

Box 63, Camp Road
Okanagan Centre, British Columbia,
Canada V0H 1P0
604-766-3168
Wine Shop: Open Daily 11AM—5PM

Gray Monk Cellars in one of the oldest and most renowned Estate Wineries in British Columbia. The Heiss family carefully selected the land for its soil conditions and microclimate that offers the aspects necessary to produce the finest wines. The winery enjoys a spectacular panoramic view of lake Okanagan and area mountains.

The majority of the grapes grown at Gray Monk come from vines that originated in Europe and now thrive under Okanagan Valley growing conditions. Pinot Gris, Pinot Blanc, Pinot Auxerrois, Kerner, Sieggerebe, and Roeberger are just a few of the over dozen grape varieties grown for Gray Monk wines.

QUAILS' GATE ESTATE WINERY

3303 Boucherie Road
Kelowna, British Columbia,
Canada V1Z 2H3
604-769-4451
800-420-9463
Open Daily for Tasting and Tours 10am–4pm

Established in 1956 by the Stewart family, Quails' Gate Estate Winery is constantly expanding. A new building is adding a 130 seat lounge/patio, new offices, expanded tank area and increased warehouse space.

In 1995, 20,000 cases were produced. Wines are separated into three ranges: Proprietor's Selection; Limited Release and Family Reserve; and Specialty Wines. This year the winery began a 10 acre per year replant program which will see the vineyard reach 100 acres planted by the year 2000.

Quails' Gate produces a range of wines including Pinot Noir, Chardonnay, Riesling, Optima, and Chasselas.

SUMAC RIDGE ESTATE WINERY

17403 Highway 97
Box 307
Summerland, British Columbia,
Canada V0H 1Z0
604-494-0451
Wine Shop & Tasting Open Year Long
Tours: Mid-May to Mid-October

In the late 1970's, the Sumac Ridge Estate Winery was born out of dreams and hard work to produce its first vintage wine in 1980. Under the guidance of proprietors Harry McWatters and Bob Wareham and Winemaker Mark Wendenburg, Sumac Ridge is into it's second decade of producing fine vinifera wines.

Sumac's own vineyards produce a wide range of grape varieties including Riesling, Gewurztraminer, Chardonnay, Pinot Blanc, Sauvignon Blanc, Merlot, Pinot Noir, Cabernet Sauvignon and Cabernet Franc.

Sumac Ridge Estate Winery was Western Canada's first producer of Methode Champenoise (Champagne) wines.

Wild Goose Vineyards and Winery

Sun Valley Way
S3 C11 RR 1
Okanagan Falls, British Columbia, Canada, V0H 1R0
604-497-8919
Winery Shop & Tasting Room: April–October: Open Daily from 10am–5pm
Off-Season: By Appointment

Wild Goose Vineyards and Winery was established in 1990 by Adolf Kruger who named his vineyards for a flock of wild Canada geese that he discovered in a clearing in the woods the day he purchased his land.

Wild Goose is classified as a Farm Gate winery that produces under 10,000 gallons yearly, producing such wines as Gewurztraminer, Johannisberg Riesling, Pinot Blanc, Pinot Noir and Marechal Foch, with the Kruger family handling all operations.

Conversion Index

Liquid Measures

1 dash	3 to 6 drops
1 teaspoon (tsp.)	⅓ tablespoon
1 tablespoon (Tbsp.)	3 teaspoons
1 tablespoon	½ fluid ounce
1 fluid ounce	2 tablespoons
1 cup	½ pint
1 cup	16 tablespoons
1 cup	8 fluid ounces
1 pint	2 cups
1 pint	16 fluid ounces

Dry Measures

1 pinch	less than ⅛ teaspoon
1 teaspoon	⅓ tablespoon
1 tablespoon	3 teaspoons
¼ cup	4 tablespoons
⅓ cup	5 tablespoons plus 1 teaspoon
½ cup	8 tablespoons
⅔ cup	10 tablespoons plus 2 teaspoons
¾ cup	12 tablespoons
1 cup	16 tablespoons

Vegetables and Fruits

Apple (1 medium)	1 cup chopped
Avocado (1 medium)	1 cup mashed
Broccoli (1 stalk)	2 cups florets
Cabbage (1 large)	10 cups, chopped
Carrot (1 medium)	½ cup, diced
Celery (3 stalks)	1 cup, diced
Eggplant (1 medium)	4 cups, cubed
Lemon (1 medium)	2 tablespoons juice
Onion (1 medium)	1 cup diced
Orange (1 medium)	½ cup juice
Parsley (1 bunch)	3 cups, chopped
Spinach (fresh), 12 cups, loosely packed	1 cup cooked
Tomato (1 medium)	¾ cup, diced
Zucchini (1 medium)	2 cups, diced

APPROXIMATE EQUIVALENTS

1 stick butter = ½ cup = 8 Tbsps. = 4 oz.
1 cup all-purpose flour = 5 oz.
1 cup cornmeal (polenta) = 4½ oz.
1 cup sugar = 8 oz.
1 cup powdered sugar = 4½ oz.
1 cup brown sugar = 6 oz.
1 large egg = 2 oz. = ¼ cup = 4 Tbsps.
1 egg yolk = 1 Tbsp. + 1 tsp.
1 egg white = 2 Tbsps. + 2 tsps.

Metric Conversion Chart

CONVERSIONS TO OUNCES TO GRAMS

To convert ounces to grams, multiply number of ounces by 28.35.

1 oz. . . . . . 30 g.	6 oz. . . . . 180 g.	11 oz. . . . 300 g.	16 oz. . . . 450 g.
2 oz. . . . . . 60 g.	7 oz. . . . . 200 g.	12 oz. . . . 340 g.	20 oz. . . . 570 g.
3 oz. . . . . . 85 g.	8 oz. . . . . 225 g.	13 oz. . . . 370 g.	24 oz. . . . 680 g.
4 oz. . . . . 115 g.	9 oz. . . . . 250 g.	14 oz. . . . 400 g.	28 oz. . . . 790 g.
5 oz. . . . . 140 g.	10 oz. . . . 285 g.	15 oz. . . . 425 g.	32 oz. . . . 900 g.

CONVERSIONS OF QUARTS TO LITERS

To convert quarts to liters, multiply number of quarts by 0.95.

1 qt. . . . . . . 1 L	2 ½ qt. . . . . 2½ L	5 qt. . . . . . 4¾ L	8 qt. . . . . . 7½ L
1½ qt. . . . . 1½ L	3 qt. . . . . . 2¾ L	6 qt. . . . . . 5½ L	9 qt. . . . . . 8½ L
2 qt. . . . . . . 2 L	4 qt. . . . . . 3¾ L	7 qt. . . . . . 6½ L	10 qt. . . . . 9½ L

CONVERSION OF FAHRENHEIT TO CELSIUS

To convert **Fahrenheit to Celsius**, subtract 32 from the Fahrenheit figure, multiply by 5, then divide by 9.

OTHER CONVERSIONS

To convert **ounces to milliliters**, multiply number of ounces by 30.
To convert **cups to liters**, multiply number of cups by 0.24.
To convert **inches to centimeters**, multiply number of inches by 2.54.

Glossary of Ingredients

ACHIOTE: a spice blend made from ground annatto seeds, garlic, cumin, vinegar and other spices.

ACORN SQUASH: a oval-shaped winter squash with a ribbed, dark-green skin and orange flesh.

ANAHEIM CHILE: elongated and cone-shaped chiles that are red or green with a mild flavor.

ANCHO CHILE: a shiny-skinned red or green cone-shaped chile with medium heat.

ARBORIO RICE: a large-grained plump rice which equires more cooking time than other rice varieties. Arborio is traditionally used for risotto because its increased starchs lend this classic dish its creamy texture.

ARMENIAN CUCUMBER: a long, pale, green-ridged cucumber with an edible skin, also known as the English cucumber.

ARUGULA: also known as rocket or roquette, noted for its strong peppery taste. Arugula makes a lively addition to salads, soups and sautéed vegetable dishes. It's a rich source of iron as well as vitamins A and C.

ASIAN NOODLES: though some Asian-style noodles are wheat-based, many others are made from ingredients such as potato flour, rice flour, buckwheat flour and yam or soybean starch.

BALSAMIC VINEGAR: made from the juice of Trebbiano grapes and traditionally aged in barrels, this tart, sweet, rich vinegar is a versatile ingredient.

BARTLETT PEAR: this large, sweet, bell-shaped fruit has a smooth, yellow-green skin that is sometimes blushed with red.

BASMATI RICE: translated as "queen of fragrance," basmati is a long-grained rice with a nutlike flavor and fine texture.

BÉCHAMEL SAUCE: a basic French white sauce made by stirring milk into a butter-flour roux. Béchamel, the base of many other sauces, was named after its inventor, Louis XIV's steward Louis de Béchamel.

BELGIAN ENDIVE: a white, yellow-edged bitter lettuce that is crunchy.

BLOOD ORANGE: a sweet-tart, thin-skinned orange with a bright red flesh.

BOK CHOY: resembles Swiss chard with its long, thick-stemmed, light green stalks. The flavor is much like cabbage.

BOUQUET GARNI: a group of herbs, such as parsley, thyme and bay leaf, that are placed in a cheesecloth bag and tied together for the use of flavor in soups, stews and broths.

BULGAR WHEAT: wheat kernels that have been steamed, dried and crushed, offering a chewy texture.

CAPERS: available in the gourmet food sections of supermarkets, capers are a small, green, pickled bud of a Mediterranean flowering plant; usually packed in brine.

CARDAMOM: a sweetly pungent, aromatic cooking spice that is a member of the ginger family.

CHANTERELLE MUSHROOM: a trumpet-shaped mushroom that resembles an umbrella turned inside out. One of the more delicious wild mushrooms.

CHÉVRE: cheese made from goat's milk is lower in fat and offers a delicate, light and slightly earthy flavor.

CHICKPEAS: also called garbanzo beans, they have a firm texture and mild, nut-like flavor. Available canned, dried or fresh.

CHICORY or CURLY ENDIVE: a crisp, curly, green-leafed lettuce. Best when young. Tend to bitter with age.

CHILE OIL: a red oil available in Asian stores. Chile oil is also easily made at home by heating 1 cup of vegetable or peanut oil with 2 dozen small dried red chiles or 1 Tbsp. cayenne.

CHIPOTLE PEPPERS: ripened and smoky-flavored jalapeño peppers have a fiery heat and delicious flavor.

CHOW-CHOW: a mustard-flavored mixed vegetable and pickle relish.

CLARIFIED BUTTER: also called drawn butter. This is an unsalted butter that has been slowly melted, thereby evaporating most of the water and separating the milk solids, which sink to the bottom of the pan. After any foam is skimmed off the top, the clear butter is poured off the milk residue and used in cooking.

COCONUT MILK: available in Asian markets, this milk is noted for its richly flavored, slightly sweet taste. Coconut milk can be made by placing 2 cups of finely grated chopped fresh coconut in 3 cups scalded milk. Stir and let stand until the milk cools to room temperature. Strain before using.

COULIS: a general term referring to a thick purée or sauce.

COURT BOUILLON: a broth made by cooking various vegetables and herbs in water.

CRÈME FRAÎCHE: a bit richer than sour cream, yet more tart than whipped heavy cream. It can be purchased in most supermarkets or made by whisking together ½ cup heavy or whipping cream, not ultra-pasteurized, with ½ cup sour cream. Pour the mixture into a jar, cover and let stand in a warm, dark area for 24 hours. This will yield 1 cup which can be kept in the refrigerator for about 10 days.

CRESS: resembles radish leaves, with a hot peppery flavor.

EGGPLANT: commonly thought of as a vegetable, eggplant is actually a fruit. The very narrow, straight Japanese or Oriental eggplant has a tender, slightly sweet flesh. The Italian or baby eggplant looks like a miniature version of the common large variety, but has a more delicate skin and flesh. The egg-shaped white eggplant makes the name of this fruit understandable.

FAVA BEANS: tan flat beans that resemble very large lima beans. Fava beans can be purchased dried, canned or fresh.

FLOWERS, EDIBLE: can be stored tightly wrapped in the refrigerator, up to a week. Some of the more popular edible flowers are the peppery-flavored nasturtiums, and chive blossoms, which taste like a mild, sweet onion. Pansies and violas offer a flavor of grapes. Some of the larger flowers such as squash blossoms can be stuffed and deep-fried.

FRISÉE: sweetest of the chicory family, with a mildly bitter taste. The leaves are a pale green, slender but curly.

FROMAGE BLANC CHEESE: fresh, day-old curds with some of the whey whipped back into the cheese. The texture is similar to ricotta cheese and is available plain or flavored.

GADO-GADO: this Indonesian favorite consists of a mixture of raw and slightly cooked vegetables served with a spicy peanut sauce.

GANACHE: a rich chocolate icing made of semisweet chocolate and whipping cream that are heated and stirred together until the chocolate has melted.

GNOCCHI: the Italian word for "dumplings," gnocchi are shaped into little balls, cooked in boiling water and served with butter and Parmesan or a savory sauce. The dough can also be chilled, sliced and either baked or fried.

GORGONZOLA CHEESE: a blue-veined Italian creamy cheese.

GRAHAM FLOUR: whole-wheat flour that is slightly coarser than the regular grind.

GRITS: coarsely ground grain such as corn, oats or rice. Grits can be cooked with water or milk by boiling or baking.

HABANERO CHILE: tiny, fat, neon orange-colored chiles that are hotter than the jalapeño chile.

HAZELNUT OIL: a lightly textured oil with a rich essence of hazelnut.

HUMMUS: this thick Middle Eastern sauce is made from mashed chickpeas seasoned with lemon juice, garlic and olive oil or sesame oil.

JALAPEÑO CHILE: these plump, thumb-size green chiles are known for wonderful flavor.

JICAMA: grows underground like a tuber, yet is part of the legume family. Beneath the thick brown skin, the flesh is creamy-white and sweet. Tastes like a cross between an apple and a potato.

KALAMATA OLIVES: intensely flavored, almond-shaped, dark purple Greek olives packed in brine.

KOSHER SALT: an additive-free, coarse-grained salt that is milder than sea salt.

LEMON GRASS: available in Asian food stores, this citrus-flavored herb has long, thin, gray-green leaves and a scallion-like base. Available fresh or dried.

LENTILS: the French or European lentil is grayish-brown with a creamy flavor. The reddish-orange Egyptian or red lentil is smaller and rounder. Lentils should be stored airtight at room temperature and will keep about 6 months. Lentils offer calcium and vitamins A and B, and are a good source of iron and phosphorus.

MÂCHE: also known as lamb's lettuce, has a delicate, sweet-nutty taste. The lettuce is a deep green.

MANGO: grows in a wide variety of shapes: oblong, kidney and round. Its thin, tough skin is green and, as the fruit ripens, becomes yellow with red mottling. Under-ripe fruit can be placed in a paper bag at room temperature.

MARJORAM: there are many species of this ancient herb, which is a member of the mint family. The most widely available is sweet marjoram or wild marjoram. Early Greeks wove marjoram into funeral wreaths and planted it on graves to symbolize their loved one's happiness, both in life and beyond.

MARSALA: a wine with a rich, smoky flavor that can range from sweet to dry.

MESCLUN: a traditional French mixture of tiny lettuces, including curly endive, red lettuce, Romaine, oak-leaf, butter lettuce and rocket.

MIRIN: a sweet cooking sake.

MISO: a fermented salty soybean paste made by crushing boiled soybeans with barley.

MOREL MUSHROOM: a wild mushroom that is cone-shaped with a spongy beige cap. Has a nutty taste.

NAPA CABBAGE: also known as Chinese cabbage, it looks like a cross between celery and lettuce, very much like romaine lettuce. The flavor is more delicate with a slight peppery taste.

NASTURTIUM FLOWERS: edible sweet and peppery flowers in a rainbow of colors. Nasturtiums are beautiful in salads and easy to grow.

NORI: paper-thin sheets of dried seaweed ranging in color from dark green to dark purple to black. Nori is rich in protein, vitamins, calcium, iron and other minerals.

OPAL BASIL: a beautiful purple basil with a pungent flavor.

OREGANO: this herb belongs to the mint family and is related to both marjoram and thyme, offering a strong, pungent flavor. Greek for "joy of the mountain," oregano was almost unheard of in the U.S. until soldiers came back from Italian World War II assignments raving about it.

OYSTER MUSHROOM: a beige fan-shaped wild mushroom with a mild flavor and soft texture.

PARMESAN CHEESE: a hard dry cheese made from skimmed or partially-skimmed cow's milk.

PECORINO CHEESE: a cheese made from sheep's milk

POLENTA: cornmeal-ground corn kernels, white or yellow, often enriched with butter and grated cheese. A staple of northern Italian cooking.

PORCINI MUSHROOM: The parasol-shaped mushroom cap has a thick stem, with a meaty, smoky flavor.

QUINOA: served like rice or as a base for salads. Pale yellow in color and slightly larger than a mustard seed with a sweet flavor and soft texture.

RADICCHIO: this peppery-tasting lettuce with brilliant, ruby-colored leaves is available year-round, with a peak season from mid-winter to early spring. Choose heads that have crisp, full-colored leaves with no sign of browning. Store in a plastic bag in the refrigerator for up to a week.

RICE WINE VINEGAR: a light, clean-tasting vinegar that works perfectly as is, in salads, as well as in a variety of Asian-inspired dishes.

RISOTTO: an Italian rice specialty made by stirring hot stock in Arborio rice that has been sautéed in butter.

ROMAINE: known for a sweet nutty flavor, this lettuce has long, crisp, green or red leaves.

ROUX: a mixture of melted butter or oil and flour used to thicken sauces, soups and stews. Sprinkle flour into the melted, bubbling-hot butter, whisking constantly over low heat, cooking at least 2 minutes.

SAFFRON: a bright yellow, strongly aromatic spice that imparts a unique flavor. Store saffron in a cool dark place for up to 6 months.

SAVOY CABBAGE: also known as curly cabbage, has lacy leaves with a white or reddish trim.

SERRANO CHILE: a fat, squat, red or green hot chile. They are milder when roasted with the ribs and seeds removed.

SHIITAKE MUSHROOM: a Japanese mushroom sold fresh or dried, which imparts a distinctively rich flavor to any dish. The versatile shiitake is suitable for almost any cooking method including sautéing, broiling and baking.

SNOW PEAS: a translucent, bright green pod that is thin, crisp and entirely edible. The tiny seeds inside are tender and sweet. Snow peas are also called Chinese snow peas and sugar peas.

SORBET: a palate refresher between courses or as a dessert, the sorbet never contains milk and often has softer consistency than sherbet.

SOY MILK: higher in protein than cow's milk, this milky, iron-rich liquid is a non-dairy product made by pressing ground, cooked soybeans. Cholesterol-free and low in calcium, fat and sodium, it makes an excellent milk substitute.

SPAGHETTI SQUASH: a yellow watermelon-shaped squash whose flesh, when cooked, separates into spaghetti-like strands.

STRUDEL: a type of pastry made up of many layers of very thin dough spread with a filling, then rolled and baked until crisp.

SUN-DRIED TOMATOES: air-dried tomatoes sold in various forms such as marinated tomato halves, which are packed in olive oil, or a tapenade, which is puréed dried tomatoes in olive oil with garlic.

TAHINI: Middle Eastern in origin, tahini is made from crushed sesame seeds. Used mainly for its creamy, rich and nutty flavor as well as for binding food together.

TEMPEH: made from cultured, fermented soybeans; comes in flat, light, grainy-looking cakes.

TOFU: a versatile fresh soybean curd, tofu is an excellent and inexpensive form of protein. It is characteristically bland in taste, but can be enhanced with seasonings.

TOMATILLOS: green husk tomatoes; small with a tart, citrus-like flavor.

TRUFFLE: a fungus that grows underground near the roots of trees prized by gourmets for centuries. Truffles should be used as soon as possible after purchase, but can be stored up to 6 days in the refrigerator or for several months in the freezer. Canned truffles, truffle paste and frozen truffles can be found in specialty stores.

VIDALIA ONION: the namesake of Vidalia, Georgia where they thrive. This yellow onion, sweet and juicy, is available in the summer or by mail- order year-round.

WATERCRESS: this spicy-flavored green is dark in color with glossy leaves.

Mail Order Sources

If you are unable to locate some of the specialty food products used in *Pacific Northwest Cooking Secrets*, you can order them from the mail order sources listed below. These items are delivered by UPS, fully insured and at reasonable shipping costs.

DRIED BEANS AND PEAS

Corti Brothers
5801 Folsom Blvd.
Sacramento, CA 95819
916-736-3800
Special gourmet items such as: imported extra-virgin olive oils, wines, exotic beans, egg pasta.

Phipps Ranch
P.O. Box 349
Pescadero, CA 94060
415-879-0787
Dried beans such as cannellini, cranberry, fava, flageolet, borlotti, scarlet runner, Tongues of Fire, and more. Also dried peas, herb vinegars, grains, herbs and spices.

DRIED MUSHROOMS

Dean & Deluca
560 Broadway
New York, NY 10012
800-221-7714
212-431-1691
Dried beans, salted capers, polenta, arborio rice, dried mushrooms, dried tomatoes, parmesan and reggiano cheeses, kitchen and baking equipment.

G.B. Ratto & Co.
821 Washington St.
Oakland, CA 94607
800-325-3483
510-836-2250 fax
Imported pasta, dried beans, amaretti cookies, semolina flour, dried mushrooms, dried tomatoes, parmesan and reggiano cheeses.

FLOURS AND GRAINS

Arrowhead Mills
Box 2059
Hereford, TX 79045
806-364-0730
A large variety of whole grain products, including specialty grains, grain mixes, flours, cereals.

Butte Creek Mill
P.O. Box 561
Eagle Point, Oregon 97524
503-826-3531
A large assortment of cereals, whole grains, rolled grains, stoneground flours and meals.

Continental Mills
P.O. Box 88176
Seattle, WA 98138
206-872-8400
Specialty whole grains, including bulgur.

Gold Mine Natural Food Co.
1947 30th St.
San Diego, CA 92102-1105
800-475-3663
Organic foods, dried foods, whole grain rice, Asian dried mushrooms, condiments, sweeteners, spices.

King Arthur Flour Baker's Catalogue
P.O. Box 876
Norwich, VT 05055
800-827-6836
Semolina flour, all types of flours, wheat berries, kitchen and baking equipment.

FRUIT & VEGETABLES

Diamond Organics
Freedom, CA 95019
800-922-2396
Free catalog available. Fresh, organically grown fruits & vegetables, specialty greens, roots, sprouts, exotic fruits, citrus, wheat grass.

Lee Anderson's Covalda Date Company
51-392 Harrison Street
(Old Highway 86)
P.O. Box 908
Coachella, CA 92236-0908
619-398-3441
Organic dates, raw date sugar and other date products. Also dried fruits, nuts and seeds.

Northwest Select
14724 184th St. NE
Arlington, WA 98223
800-852-7132
206-435-8577
Fresh baby artichokes.

Timber Crest Farms
4791 Dry Creek Road
Healdsburg, CA 95448
707-433-8251
Domestic dried tomatoes and other unsulfured dried fruits and nuts.

SEEDS FOR GROWING HERBS AND VEGETABLES

Shepherd's Garden Seeds
6116 Highway 9
Felton, CA 95018
408-335-6910
Excellent selection of vegetable and herb seeds with growing instructions.

The Cook's Garden
P.O. Box 535
Londonderry, VT 05148
802-824-3400
Organically grown, reasonably priced vegetable, herb and flower seeds. Illustrated catalog has growing tips and recipes.

W. Atlee Burpee & Co.
Warminster, PA 18974
800-888-1447
Well-known, reliable, full-color seed catalog.

SPECIALTY FOODS AND FOOD GIFTS

China Moon Catalogue
639 Post St.
San Francisco, CA 94109
415-771-MOON (6666)
415-775-1409 fax
Chinese oils, peppers, teas, salts, beans, candied ginger, kitchen supplies, cookbooks.

Corti Brothers
5801 Folsom Blvd.
Sacramento, CA 95819
916-736-3800
Special gourmet items such as: imported extra-virgin olive oils, wines, exotic beans, egg pasta.

Gazin's Inc.
P.O. Box 19221
New Orleans, LA 70179
504-482-0302
Specializing in Cajun, Creole and New Orleans foods.

Kozlowski Farms
5566 Gravenstein Highway
Forestville, CA 95436
707-887-1587
800-473-2767
Jams, jellies, barbecue and steak sauces, conserves, honeys, salsas, chutneys and mustards. Some products are non-sugared, others are in the organic line. You can customize your order from 65 different products.

Williams-Sonoma
Mail Order Dept.
P.O. Box 7456
San Francisco,
CA 94120-7456
800-541-2233
credit card orders
800-541-1262
customer service
Vinegars, oils, foods and kitchenware.

SPICES AND HERBS

Fox Hill Farm
444 West Michigan Avenue
P.O.Box 9
Parma, MI 49269
517-531-3179
Fresh-cut herb plants, topiaries, ornamental and medicinal herbs.

Nichols Garden Nursery
1190 N. Pacific Hwy
Albany, OR 97321
503-928-9280
Fresh herb plants.

Old Southwest Trading Company
P.O.Box 7545
Albuquerque, NM 87194
800-748-2861
505-831-5144
Specializes in chiles, everything from dried chiles to canned chiles and other chile-related products.

Penzey Spice House Limited
P.O. Box 1633
Milwaukee, WI 53201
414-768-8799
Fresh ground spices (saffron, cinnamon and peppers), bulk spices, seeds, and seasoning mixes.

Recipe Index

Final Temptations

About the Author

KATHLEEN DEVANNA FISH, author of the popular "Secrets" series, is a gourmet cook and gardener who is always on the lookout for recipes with style and character.

In addition to *Pacific Northwest Cooking Secrets,* Kathleen has written the award-winning *Great Vegetarian Cookbook, Cooking Secrets for Healthy Living, The Gardener's Cookbook, The Great California Cookbook, California Wine Country Cooking Secrets, San Francisco's Cooking Secrets, Monterey's Cooking Secrets, New England's Cooking Secrets, Cape Cod's Cooking Secrets,* and *Cooking and Traveling Inn Style.*

Before embarking on a writing and publishing career, she owned and operated three businesses in the travel and hospitality industry.

ROBERT FISH, award-winning photojournalist, produces the images that bring together the concept of the "Secrets" series.

In addition to taking the cover photographs, Robert explores the food and wine of each region, helping to develop the overview upon which each book is based.

Bon Vivant Press

A division of The Millennium Press
P.O. Box 1994
Monterey, CA 93942
800-524-6826
408-373-0592
408-373-3567 FAX

Send ________ copies of *Pacific Northwest Cooking Secrets* at $15.95 each.

Send ________ copies of *Cooking for Healthy Living* at $15.95 each.

Send ________ copies of *The Great California Cookbook* at $15.95 each.

Send ________ copies of *The Gardener's Cookbook* at $15.95 each.

Send ________ copies of *The Great Vegetarian Cookbook* at $15.95 each.

Send ________ copies of *California Wine Country Cooking Secrets* at $14.95 each.

Send ________ copies of *San Francisco's Cooking Secrets* at $13.95 each.

Send ________ copies of *Monterey's Cooking Secrets* at $13.95 each.

Send ________ copies of *New England's Cooking Secrets* at $14.95 each.

Send ________ copies of *Cape Cod's Cooking Secrets* at $14.95 each.

Send ________ copies of *Jewish Cooking Secrets From Here and Far* at $14.95 each.

Add $3.00 postage and handling for the first book ordered and $1.50 for each additional book. Please add $1.08 sales tax per book, for those books shipped to California addresses.

Please charge my ☐ Visa ☐ MasterCard #________________________________

Expiration date Signature ________________________

Enclosed is my check for________________________________

Name________________________________

Address________________________________

City State Zip____________

☐ This is a gift. Send directly to:

Name________________________________

Address________________________________

City State Zip____________

☐ Autographed by the author
Autographed to ________________________________

NOTES